LEED® v3 and BD&C Study Guide

Summary of LEED v3 and BD&C Prerequisites and Credits

Charles C. Passman, PE, CEM, LEED AP
Certified Green Building Engineer

LEED® v3 and BD&C Study Guide:
Summary of LEED v3 and BD&C Prerequisites and Credits

Current printing of this edition: 1

Printing History______________________

edition number	printing number	update __
1	1	New book

Printed in the United States of America

ISBN: 978-0-615-31202-6

BD&C Prerequisites and Points List for NC, Schools and C&S
(Shading indicates variation from NC prerequisites and/or Pts)

Credit	NC	Schools	C&S
SS Pr 1	Reqd	Required	Reqd
SS Pr 2	NA	Reqd	NA
SS Cr 1	1	1	1
SS Cr 2	5	4	5
SS Cr 3	1	1	1
SS Cr 4.1	6	4	6
SS Cr 4.2	1	1	2
SS Cr 4.3	3	2	3
SS Cr 4.4	2	2	2
SS Cr 5.1	1	1	1
SS Cr 5.2	1	1	1
SS Cr 6.1	1	1	1
SS Cr 6.2	1	1	1
SS Cr 7.1	1	1	1
SS Cr 7.2	1	1	1
SS Cr 8	1	1	1
SS Cr 9	NA	NA	1
SS Cr 9	NA	1	NA
SS Cr 10	NA	1	NA
SS Total	**26**	**24**	**28**
WE Pr 1	Reqd	Required	Reqd
WE Cr 1	2-4	2-4	2-4
WE Cr 2	2	2	2
WE Cr 3	2-4	2-4	2-4
WE Cr 4	NA	1	NA
WE Total	**6-10**	**7-11**	**6-10**
EA Pr 1	Reqd	Required	Reqd
EA Pr 2	Reqd	Required	Reqd
EA Pr 3	Reqd	Required	Reqd
EA Cr 1	1-19	1-19	3-21
EA Cr 2	1-7	1-7	4
EA Cr 3	2	2	2
EA Cr 4	2	1	2
EA Cr 5	3	2	NA
EA Cr 5.1	NA	NA	3
EA Cr 5.2	NA	NA	3
EA Cr 6	2	2	2
EA Total	**11-35**	**9-33**	**19-37**

Credit	NC	Schools	C&S
MR Pr 1	Reqd	Required	Reqd
MR Cr 1.1	1-3	1-2	NA
MR Cr 1	NA	NA	1-5
MR Cr 1.2	1	1	NA
MR Cr 2	1-2	1-2	1-2
MR Cr 3	1-2	1-2	1
MR Cr 4	1-2	1-2	1-2
MR Cr 5	1-2	1-2	1-2
MR Cr 6	1	1	NA
MR Cr 7	1	1	NA
MR Cr 6	NA	NA	1
MR Total	**8-14**	**8-13**	**6-13**
IEQ Pr 1	Reqd	Required	Reqd
IEQ Pr 2	Reqd	Required	Reqd
IEQ Pr 3	NA	Required	NA
IEQ Cr 1	1	1	1
IEQ Cr 2	1	1	1
IEQ Cr 3.1	1	1	NA
IEQ Cr 3	NA	NA	1
IEQ Cr 3.2	1	1	NA
IEQ Cr 4.1	1	1	1
IEQ Cr 4.2	1	1	1
IEQ Cr 4.3	1	1	1
IEQ Cr 4.4	1	1	1
IEQ Cr 4.5	NA	***	NA
IEQ Cr 4.6	NA	***	NA
IEQ Cr 5	1	1	1
IEQ Cr 6.1	1	1	NA
IEQ Cr 6.2	1	1	NA
IEQ Cr 6	NA	NA	1
IEQ Cr 7.1	1	1	NA
IEQ Cr 7	NA	NA	1
IEQ Cr 7.2	1	1	NA
IEQ Cr 8.1	1	1-3	1
IEQ Cr 8.2	1	1	1
IEQ Cr 9	NA	1	NA
IEQ Cr 10	NA	1	NA
***Schools choose four from 4.1-4.6**			
IEQ Total	**15**	**17-19**	**12**
ID Cr 1	1-5	1-4	1-5
ID Cr 2	1	1	1
ID Cr 3	NA	1	NA
ID Total	**2-6**	**3-6**	**2-6**
Regional Priority Credit 1 (RP Cr 1)	**1-4**	**1-4**	**1-4**
Total Bonus Credits Available	**3-10**	**4-10**	**3-10**

Certification Level	Points Required
Certified	40
Silver	50
Gold	60
Platinum	80
Base Total	**100**
Bonus Total	**10**
Total	**110**

Credits for Which Exemplary Performance Points are Available

SS Credit 2	**Development Density and Community**
SS Credit 4	**Alternative Transportation**
SS Credit 5	**Site Development**
SS Credit 6	**Stormwater Design**
SS Credit 7	**Heat Island**
SS Credit 10	**Joint Use of Facilities (Schools only)**
WE Credit 2	**Innovative Wastewater Technologies**
WE Credit 3	**Water Use Reduction**
WE Credit 4	**Process Water Use Reduction (Schools only)**
EA Credit 1	**Optimize Energy Performance**
EA Credit 2	**On-site Renewable Energy**
EA Credit 3	**Enhanced Commissioning**
EA Credit 6	**Green Power**
MR Credit 1	**Building Reuse: Maintain Existing Walls, Floors and Roof (C&S only)**
MR Credit 2	**Construction Waste Management**
MR Credit 3	**Materials Reuse**
MR Credit 4	**Recycled Content**
MR Credit 5	**Regional Materials**
MR Credit 6	**Rapidly Renewable Materials (New Construction and Schools only)**
MR Credit 7	**Certified Wood (C&S, MR Credit 6)**
IEQ Credit 3	**Construction Indoor Air Quality Management Plan (C&S)**
IEQ Credit 8	**Daylight and Views**
IEQ Credit 9	**Enhanced Acoustical Performance (Schools only)**
IEQ Credit 10	**Mold Prevention (Schools only)**

LEED Version 3: Building Design and Construction

- **LEED is a certification program initiated by the USGBC (US Green Building Council).**

- Buildings annually consume over 60% of the electricity and over 30% of the total energy used in the U.S.

- In 2006, the commercial sector produced more than 1 billion metric tons of CO2, more than a 30% increase over 1990.

- 5 billion gallons of potable water per day are used just to flush toilets.

- 1.6 pounds of solid waste per day are produced by a typical North American commercial building employee.

- Green building practices reduce/eliminate negative environmental impacts, reduce O&M costs, enhance marketability, increase workers' productivity and reduce potential liability from IAQ problems.

- LEED AP Specialties and Rating Systems:

LEED VERSION 3

LEED AP Specialities:

BD+C	**Building Design & Construction**
ID+C	**Interior Design & Construction**
O+M	**Existing Building: Operation & Maintenance**
Homes	**Home Design & Construction**
ND	**Neighborhood Planning & Development**

LEED Rating Systems	**Reference Guide**
New Construction	**Green Building Design & Construction 2009**
Core and Shell	**Green Building Design & Construction 2009**
Schools	**Green Building Design & Construction 2009**
Existing Buildings: O&M	**Green Building Operations & Maintenance 2009**
Commercial Interiors	**Green Interior Design & Construction 2009**
Future:	
Healthcare	**Green Building Design & Construction**
Retail Interiors	**Green Interior Design & Construction**
Existing Schools	**Green Building Operations & Maintenance**
Homes	**Coming 2011**
Neighborhood Development	**Coming 2009**

- LEED Version 3 consists of the following:
  1. LEED 2009
  2. LEED Online
  3. Certification Model

- LEED addresses the following: **Sustainable Sites (SS), Water Efficiency (WE), Energy & Atmosphere (EA), Materials & Resources (MR), Indoor Environmental Quality (EQ), Innovation in Design (ID) and Regional Priority (RP).**

- Until June 27, 2009, projects have the option to apply under **LEED-NC 2.2 or LEED 2009.**

- The Green Building Certification Institute (GBCI) administers credentialing, and project registration and certification.

- A viable project must meet all the Prerequisites and achieve the minimum Credit points required for certification.

- Products cannot be LEED certified, although they can contribute to the achievement of a Credit point.

- **Innovation in Design (ID) Credits: Exemplary Performance** – double credit requirements or achieve the next incremental percentage threshold; **Innovative Strategies** – those not addressed by the LEED rating system and demonstrate significant and quantifiable environmental and/or health benefits.

- **100 Credits and 4 levels: 40% for Certified, 50% for Silver, 60% for Gold, 80% for Platinum**
- 10 Bonus Points add to the tally but not toward the next level: 6 for ID, 4 for RP,
- A maximum of 3 of the possible 6 ID points may be allotted as Exemplary Performance ID points

- Registration fee for members/non-members: $450/$600
- Certification fees for members/non-members for GBD&C and GID&C buildings through 12/31/2009:

Minimum	50K-500K sq ft	Maximum
$1,750/$2,250	$.035/$.045	$17,500/$22,500

- Certification fees for members/non-members for GBD&C and GID&C buildings effective 1/1/2010:

Minimum	50K-500K sq ft	Maximum
$2,250/$2,750	$.045/$.055	$22,500/$27,500

- The fee for an Expedited Certification is $10,000 in addition to the regular fee, regardless of building size.

- GBCI will proceed with application review when all project documentation and payments have been received and processed.

- Registration fees, appeal review fees and any additional fees required to expedite LEED certification are not refundable.

- Appeals: may be filed after the design phase review or the final review at $500 per Credit or Prerequisite.

USGBC Website - LEED APs, Project Certification, Resources:

- **LEED AP: Valuable and marketable credential for employers, prospective employers, or clients**
- Registration: Learn about the registration process and how to register your project for LEED certification.
- Certification: Learn about the LEED certification process and how to use LEED-Online.
- LEED-Online: LEED information, resources, and support - Project team members can upload data and documentation, view and submit Credit Interpretation Requests, manage key project details, and view and respond to reviewer comments.
- Portfolio Program: Learn about USGBC's Portfolio Program, which supports building owners working to earn LEED certification by providing a cost-effective, streamlined certification process.
- Credit Interpretation Requests (CIRs): Project applicants seeking technical and administrative guidance on how LEED credits apply to their projects can find guidelines, search existing credit interpretation rulings, or submit a new credit interpretation request.
- LEED Project Directory: Search for LEED-certified and registered projects in your area.
- LEED AP Directory: Search for LEED Accredited Professionals in your area.
- Government Resources: Relevant documents and public policies.

History of LEED:

- **1993: LEED formed out of necessity to develop a system to define and measure Green Buildings**
- **1998: LEED 1.0 launched as a standard for defining and measure Green Buildings**
- **2000: LEED 2.0 released as the LEED Green Building Rating System**
- **2009: LEED Version 3 launched**
- **2009: June 27 – New projects required to register for LEED 2009**
- **2009: December 31 – Last day for free upgrades to LEED v3 for existing projects**

Features of LEED:

- **Voluntary, Consensus-based, Market-driven.**
- Whole building perspective over a building's life cycle.
- Provides a definitive standard for green building design, construction and operation.
- Rating system organized into 5 environmental categories.
- Innovation in Design (ID) bonus points address sustainable expertise and design measures not covered.
- Regional Priority (RP) bonus points acknowledge importance of local conditions in determining best environmental practices.

LEED Credit Weightings:

- **In LEED 2009, point allocation to credits is based on the <u>potential environmental impacts and human benefits</u> of each with respect to a set of <u>impact categories</u>: greenhouse gas emissions, fossil fuel use, toxins and carcinogens, air and water pollutants, indoor environmental conditions.**
- Energy modeling, life-cycle assessment and transportation analysis are used in combination to quantify each type of impact.
- **Credit Weighting** is the allocation of points among credits.
- LEED 2009 uses the U.S. EPA's **TRACI** (<u>T</u>ools for the <u>R</u>eduction and <u>A</u>ssessment of <u>C</u>hemical and Other Environmental <u>I</u>mpacts) environmental impact categories as the basis for weighting each credit.
- TRACI helps evaluate impacts for life-cycle assessment, industrial ecology, process design and pollution prevention.
- LEED 2009 also uses weightings developed by the **NIST** (National Institute of Standards and Technology).
- TRACI and the NIST are used to compare impact categories with one another and assign relative weight to each.
- Each credit is allocated points based on the relative importance of the building-related impacts that it addresses.
- The weighted average combines building impacts and the relative value of the impact categories.
- Credits that most directly address the most important impacts are given the greatest weight.
- The LEED 2009 changes in point allocation reflect the relative emphasis on the reduction of energy consumption and greenhouse gas emissions.
- Each rating system is unique in the portion of the environmental footprint addressed and the relative allocation of points.
- The LEED credit weighting process is based on the following parameters:

  1. All credits are worth a minimum of 1 point.
  2. All credits are positive whole numbers.
  3. All credits receive a single, static weight in each rating system.
  4. All rating systems have 100 base points and up to 10 bonus points (ID or RP).

- The LEED credit weighting process involves 3 steps:

  1. A reference building is used to estimate the environmental impacts in 13 categories.
  2. The relative importance of building impacts in each category are set to reflect values based on the NIST weightings.
  3. Points are assigned to credits based on data that quantify building impacts on environmental health and human health.

Minimum Program Requirements

- A project must adhere to LEED's Minimum Program Requirements (MPRs) which evolve over time with the rating systems.
- These requirements define the categories of buildings that the rating systems are design to evaluate and serve 3 goals:

  1. Give clear guidance to customers.
  2. Protect the integrity of the LEED program.
  3. Reduce challenges that occur during the certification process.

When to Use LEED for New Construction

- All commercial buildings, as defined by standard building codes, are eligible for certification as LEED for NC buildings.
- LEED for NC addresses design and construction activities for both new buildings and major renovations of existing buildings.
- A major renovation involves major HVAC renovation, significant envelope modifications and major interior rehabilitation.
- The owner or tenant must occupy more than 50% of the building's leasable sq. ft., otherwise use LEED for C&S.

When to Use LEED for Core & Shell

- LEED for C&S acknowledges the limited level of influence a developer can exert in a speculatively developed building.
- LEED for C&S serves the speculative development market in which project teams do not control all scopes of a whole building's design and construction.
- LEED for C&S can be used for projects in which the developer controls the entire core and shell but not the tenant fit-out.
- The owner must occupy 50% or less of the building's leasable sq. ft.
- Project teams should review the following GBD&C Reference Guide Core and Shell appendixes:

    1. App 1 – Default Occupancy Counts: for determining full-time equivalent (FTE) and transient occupants
    2. App 2 – C&S Energy Modeling Guidelines: how to model building systems that are beyond the developer's scope of work
    3. App 3 – C&S Project Scope: a checklist for certification/precertication showing portions of work within developer's control
    4. App 4 – Tenant Lease or Sales Agreement: allows developers to achieve credits thru a binding lease or sales agreement
    5. App 5 – C&S Precertification Guidance: signifies commitment and enables marketing of advantages to potential tenants

When to Use LEED for Schools

- LEED for Schools addresses both new school buildings and major renovations of existing school buildings.
- LEED for Schools must be used for academic buildings on K-12 grounds; other buildings on a school campus are eligible for 2 or more LEED rating system project scopes, e.g. LEED for Schools and LEED for NC.

LEED Online

- All project teams are required to use LEED Online.
- LEED Online is the primary resource for managing the LEED documentation process.
- LEED Online is used to manage project details, complete documentation requirements for prerequisites and credits, upload supporting data, submit applications for review, receive reviewer feedback, and earn certification.
- LEED Online support capabilities enable team members to view and submit Credit Interpretation Requests (CIRs), contact customer service, generate project-specific reports and consult supplementary LEED resources.
- LEED Certificates are issued through LEED Online.

Credit Interpretation Requests and Rulings

- A credit interpretation may be requested if the reference guide doesn't sufficiently address a specific issue or a conflict requires resolution; a credit interpretation ruling process has been established for each LEED rating system.
- CIRs must be submitted online as follows:

    1. Read previously posted CIRs and responses.
    2. If no relevant CIR exists, submit the request.
    3. The CIR can be circulated.
    4. The inquiry and ruling must be submitted with the LEED application.
    5. Do's:
        - Be brief but explicit.
        - Base the CIR on the applicable Rating System and Reference Guide.
        - Place special emphasis on the **Intent** of the Prerequisite or Credit.
        - Offer potential solutions to the problem.
        - Solicit approval or rejection of your proposed interpretation.
    6. Don'ts:
        - Don't state a credit name or conflict.
        - Don't include any confidential details.
        - Don't format the CIR as a letter.
        - Don't reference more than one Prerequisite or Credit.
        - Don't include any lengthy narratives.
        - Don't include any attachments.
    7. Cost: **$220 per CIR**

LEED Online Documentation Requirements

- Certification applications must include the required LEED Online documentation: general documentation, documentation for all prerequisites, and documentation for all pursued credits.
- **General Documentation Requirements** include submission of an overall project narrative with the completed LEED Online documentation requirements; the narrative describes the applicant's organization, building, site and team.
- **General Documentation Requirements** also include the basic details pertaining to project site conditions, construction scope and timeline, occupant usage data and project team identification. Any optional descriptions may be included.

Credit Substitution

- LEED 2009 rating systems do not allow credit substitution using another version.

LEED for Core & Shell <u>Precertification</u> Application

- Precertification is formal recognition by GBCI that the owner/developer has established LEED for C&S certification as a goal.
- It is unique to LEED for C&S and projects may or may not pursue at their discretion.
- It gives C&S owners/developers a marketing tool to attract potential tenants and financiers.
- It occurs early in the design process and is **based on declared goals and intent, not actual achievement**.
- Project teams must confirm that the project intends to meet the requirements of a credit.
- The project team's documentation and GBCI's review is less vigorous and comprehensive.
- Precertification is not required for a documented and completed building.
- Precertification is not confirmation of or a commitment to achieving LEED for C&S certification.
- It is not LEED Certification.

LEED for NC, Schools and C&S <u>Certification</u> Application

- Designate a Team Leader to manage the compilation of documentation throughout design and construction.
- The certification application **may be split into two phases: design and construction**.
- Register the Project

    1. Establish contact with USGBC.
    2. Obtain information on registration costs.
    3. Obtain access to the LEED-Online project tool, errata, critical communications & essential information.

- The individual who initially registers the project will be identified as the **Project Administrator**.
- The Project Administrator may be substituted at any time.
- Other registrants (team members) will be listed as users and will have limited capacity, e.g. access and enter information.
- **Only the Project Administrator may submit an application for review.**
- Application: Design Phase and Construction Phase, or combine for Review at Substantial Completion.

    1. **Design Phase Review**
        a) Submit design phase application and design phase fee (portion of total certification fee).
        b) USGBC formally rules each attempted credit as <u>"Anticipated"</u> or "Denied".
        c) No certification or credit is awarded.
        d) Likelihood of credit achievement is assessed if design is executed according to specifications.
    2. **Construction Phase Review**
        a) Submit all credits for review at completion of construction and pay remainder of fee.
        b) Submit documents to substantiate credit compliance for any <u>changes in "Anticipated"</u> credits.
        c) Submit verification that unchanged "Anticipated" credit design has been executed as required.
        d) Ruling will declare "Anticipated" as "Achieved" credits and all others as "Achieved" or "Denied"

- Receive Formal Letter of Certification and Plaque.
- Appeals: $500 per Prereq/Credit, reviewed within 25 business days, reviewed by a different team.

Timeline of Project Phases

1. **Predesign:** gather information, recognize stakeholder needs and establish project goals.
2. **Schematic Design:** explore several design options and alternatives.
3. **Design Development:** begin the process of spatial refinement; involves the first design of the energy systems.
4. **Construction Documents:** carry the design to the level of details for all spaces, systems and materials.
5. **Construction**
6. **Substantial completion:** contractual benchmark at which a client can occupy a nearly completed space.
7. **Final Completion**
8. **Certification:** recognition by a local building department that the building conforms to building safety codes.

Exemplary Performance Strategies

- A type of ID point; **only three of a possible six ID points can be Exemplary Performance points.**
- Performance that greatly exceeds the performance level or expands the scope required by an existing credit.
- The project must meet the performance level defined by the next step in the threshold progression.
- For credits with multiple compliance paths, an ID point can be earned by satisfying more than 1 path if benefits are additive.
- The available exemplary performance points are indicated in LEED Online and in the reference guides by the "ribbon" logo.

Regional Priority Credits

- RP credits allow bonus points for addressing geographically specific environmental issues.
- Projects may achieve **four of a possible 6 RP points** (1 point per eligible credit) per rating system.
- LEED Online automatically determines a project's RP credits.

Registered Project Tools Website

- **Resources for starting projects:** errata for each rating system, documentation requirements, referenced industry standards.
- **Declarant definitions:** team member responsibilities (prerequisites, credits, documentation requirement sign offs); the required declarant is noted in the corresponding credit documentation section of LEED Online.
- **Licensed Professional Exemption Form:**
  - Used by the team's registered PE, registered architect or registered landscape architect as a streamlined path to certain credits, thereby bypassing otherwise required submittals.
  - Used in conjunction with the declarations in LEED Online to document any exemptions.
  - Required for any eligible submittal requirements the project team wishes to waive.
  - Noted in the corresponding credit documentation of LEED Online.

LEED for Green Building Design and Construction Reference Guide

- Presents criteria for achieving prerequisites, credits and certification.
- Provides the reasoning behind the criteria.
- Provides strategies for implementation.
- Provides documentation requirements.
- Provides examples of strategies, case studies and additional resources.
- Does not provide an exhaustive list of strategies or all the information necessary to determine applicability of a credit.

Prerequisite and Credit Format

Intent	**Calculations**
Requirements	**Documentation Guidance**
Benefits and Issues to Consider	**Examples**
Related Credits	**Exemplary Performance**
Summary of Referenced Standards	**Regional Variations**
Implementation	**Resources**
Timeline and Team	**Definitions**

Sustainable Sites (SS) `NC 26 Pts, Schools 24 Pts, C&S 28 Pts`

- SS credits address environmental concerns related to building landscape, hardscape and exterior building issues.
- SS credits promote responsible, innovative, practical strategies that are sensitive to plants, wildlife and water and air quality.
- SS credits mitigate some of the negative effects buildings have on the local and regional environment.
- For single-building developments, the submittal covers the entire project scope and is generally limited to the site boundary.
- If a project is a portion of a multiple-building development, the project boundary is the portion of the project that is submitted for certification and must be used consistently across all SS prerequisites and credits.

SS credits promote the following measures:

Select and Develop the Site Wisely
- Development of a greenfield (previously undeveloped site) <u>consumes land</u>.
- Development projects may encroach on agricultural lands/wetlands/water bodies and <u>compromise existing wildlife habitats</u>.
- Choose previously developed or damaged sites, develop a project site master plan, and plan for joint use of facilities.

Reduce Emissions Associated with Transportation
- In 2006, 76% of commuters in the US ages 16 and older drove to work alone.
- Of the remaining 24% who used alternative transportation (incl. work at home), 11% carpooled and 5% used public transport.

Plant Sustainable Landscapes
- Sustainable practices minimize the use of irrigation, fertilizers and pesticides.
- Sustainable practices can prevent soil erosion and sedimentation.

Protect Surrounding Habitats
- Building sites can encroach on agricultural lands and adversely affect wildlife habitat.
- Preserve and restore native and adapted vegetation and ecological features to provide wildlife habitat.

Manage Stormwater Runoff
- Projects reduce surface permeability and increase runoff transported via pipes and sewers to streams, rivers, & water bodies.
- Projects may cause stormwater runoff that harms water quality, aquatic life and humans in the receiving waters.
- Control, reduce and treat stormwater runoff before it leaves the project site.

Reduce Heat Island Effect
- Use of dark, nonreflective surfaces contributes to the heat island effect by absorption (of solar radiation) and radiation.
- 1/6 of the electricity consumed in the US is used to cool buildings.
- Install reflective surfaces and vegetation.

Eliminate Light Pollution
- Light pollution can interfere with nocturnal ecology, reduce sky observation, cause roadway glare and bother neighbors.
- Pollution reduction encourages nocturnal wildlife to inhabit the site and lessens disruption of birds' migratory patterns.
- Exterior lighting strategies may reduce infrastructure costs and energy use over the life of the building.

		Rainfall	Runoff	
1.	**Humid Watershed**	$\geq$ 40" per year	1" rain	(equivalent to treating 90% of average rainfall event)
2.	**Semi-arid Watershed**	= 20" – 40" per year	¾" rain	(equivalent to treating 90% of average rainfall event)
3.	**Arid Watershed**	< 20" per year	½" rain	(equivalent to treating 90% of average rainfall event)

SRI:	Calculated according to ASTM E 1980
Reflectance:	Calculated according to ASTM E 903, E 1918 or C 1549
Emittance:	Calculated according to ASTM E 408, or C 1371

Standard Black Surface:	R = 0.05, E = 0.9	SRI = 0
Standard White Surface:	R = 0.80, E = 0.9	SRI = 100

SS Prerequisite 1 Construction Activity Pollution Prevention

Intent: Reduce pollution from construction activities by controlling soil erosion, waterway sedimentation and airborne dust generation.

Requirements: Create and implement an Erosion and Sedimentation Control (**ESC**) Plan, conforming to 2003 EPA Construction General Permit (**CGP**) or local standards/codes, to accomplish the following objectives:

1. Prevent soil erosion from runoff and/or wind erosion, including stockpiling topsoil for reuse.
2. Prevent sedimentation of storm sewer or receiving streams.
3. Prevent polluting of air with dust and particulate matter.

Technology and Strategy:

- Applies to ALL size projects.
- Design phase ESC Plan conforming to 2003 CGP.
- CGP conforms to Phase I and II of National Pollutant Discharge Elimination System (**NPDES**) program.
- Consider <u>stabilization measures</u>: seeding (temporary and permanent) and mulching.
- Consider <u>structural measures</u>: dikes, silt fence, sediment traps and basins.
- On-site: topsoil loss is the most significant environmental issue.
- Off-site: water quality and sedimentation are the most significant environmental issues.

Eutrophication: increase in chemical nutrients in an ecosystem, e.g. N & P found in fertilizers.
NPDES: controls water pollution by regulating point sources of pollutant discharge.
Sedimentation: addition of soil particles to water bodies by nature or humans.
Stormwater Runoff: rain that leaves the project site boundary on the surface & flows into the sewer or receiving bodies of water.

Calculations: na

Exemplary Performance: na

Construction Submittal

Timeline/Team: Design phase – Civil Engineer or Landscape Arch; Construction Phase – Civil Engineer, Landscape Arch, GC.

Regional Variations: Adhere to either local standards and codes or 2003 EPA CGP, whichever is more stringent.

O&M Considerations: Plan for permanent erosion control measures and periodic visual inspections.

SS Prerequisite 2 Environmental Site Assessment (Schools only)

Intent: Ensure that the site is assessed for environmental contamination and if contaminated, that the environmental contamination has been remediated to protect children's health.

Requirements:

- Conduct a Phase I Environmental Site Assessment (per ASTM E1527-05) to determine if environmental contamination exists.
- Conduct a Phase II Environmental Site Assessment (per ASTM E1903-97,2002).
- **School sites that are contaminated by past use as a landfill are ineligible for LEED certification.**
- If a site is otherwise contaminated, it must be remediated per local, state or federal EPA regional residential (unrestricted) standards, whichever is most stringent.
- Documentation from the authority must be provided to prove that safe levels of contamination have been achieved.
- **SS Cr 3 (Brownfield Redevelopment) can be achieved through successful documented remediation of the site.**

Environmental Issues: Students have numerous opportunities to come in direct with soil.

Economic Issues: Phase I assessments are often required by lenders. Phase II assessments and remediation can be costly, but these costs can be offset by lower property costs.

Technology and Strategy:

- Conduct a <u>Phase I</u> assessment with the assistance of remediation experts with <u>no testing of soil, water or air</u>:
  1. Review historical records related to the site.
  2. Visit the site to identify potential features or elements that may indicate the presence of hazardous materials.
  3. Interview people who know the site's history and use, e.g. owners/managers, government officials or neighbors.
- Conduct a Phase II assessment if Phase I finds reasons to suspect contaminants and recommends further testing.
- <u>Phase II</u>: collect samples to be analyzed for <u>petroleum hydrocarbons, heavy metals, solvents, pesticides, asbestos and mold</u>.
- Remediation: Pump-and-treat, bioreactors, land farming, in situ remediation.
- <u>Use EPA Region 9 cleanup standards</u> since they are the most appropriate <u>for protecting children's health and safety</u>.

Calculations: na

Exemplary Performance: na

Construction Submittal

Timeline/Team: Site selection process – environmental professionals, state/local regulators, EPA.

Regional Variations: Preliminary screening levels or remediation criteria may differ from relative EPA standards.

O&M Considerations: Keep careful records of any remediation and develop a plan for ongoing compliance with monitoring and reporting requirements of the relevant local, state or federal regulatory agency.

SS Credit 1 Site Selection (NC 1 Point, Schools 1 Point, C&S 1 Point)

Intent: Avoid development of inappropriate sites and reduce the environmental impact from the location of a building on a site.

Requirements: Do not develop buildings, hardscape, roads or parking areas on portions of sites that meet any one of the following criteria:

1. <u>Prime farmland</u> as defined by the US Dept of Agriculture.
2. Previously undeveloped land with <u>elevation < 5' above the elevation of the 100-year flood (1%/yr, not worst in 100 yrs)</u>.
3. Habitat for any species on Federal or State <u>threatened or endangered</u> lists.
4. <u>Within 100' of wetlands</u> (Fed, state or local) <u>or within setback distances from wetlands</u> (state or local).
5. Previously undeveloped land within <u>50' of a water body</u> (natural and can support fish, recreation or industrial use).
6. <u>Public parkland</u> unless land of equal or greater is traded to public land owner (Park Authority projects are exempt).

Technology and Strategy:

- A Qualified professional should survey the site and inventory important environmental characteristics.
- Give preference to sites that do not include sensitive site elements and restrictive land types.
- Design the building with the minimal footprint to minimize disruption to environmentally sensitive areas.

Development Footprint: Hardscape, access roads, parking lots, non-building facilities and the building itself.

Calculations: na

Exemplary Performance: na

Design Submittal

Environmental Impact: Habitat Preservation

Economic Impact: Public Response and Involvement

Timeline/Team: Landscape Architect, Ecologist, Environmental Engineer, Civil Engineer, local professionals.

Regional Variations: na

O&M Considerations: environmentally sensitive areas should be labeled and protected.

SS Credit 2 Development Density and Community Connectivity (5, 4, 5)

Intent: Channel development to urban areas with existing infrastructure, protect greenfields and preserve habitat and natural resources.

Requirements:

OPTION 1 – DEVELOPMENT DENSITY

- **Construct or renovate a building on a previously developed site.**
- **Site must be in a community with minimum Development Density of <u>60,000 ft^2/ac</u> net.**
- <u>**Schools**</u>: **Phys ed. fields/playgrounds and concession stands are excluded from the development density calcs.**

OPTION 2 – COMMUNITY CONNECTIVITY

- Construct or renovate a building on a previously developed site, **AND**
- Within ½ mile from a residential area/neighborhood with an average density of 10 units/ac, **AND**
- Within ½ mile radius from [**a main NC & CS**] [<u>**any** School</u>] building entrance to at least **10 Basic Services**.
- Nor more than 2 of the 10 services may be anticipated, i.e. **8 of 10 must be existing and operational**.
- For <u>mixed use projects</u>, only 1 service within the project boundary may be 1 of the ten, <u>provided it is open to the public</u>.

Technology and Strategy:
- Give preference to urban sites with pedestrian access to a variety of services

Property Density = Building Density, must be minimum of <u>60,000 ft^2/ac</u>
Development Density = average property density within the Density Boundary
Site area includes area of project being built and is based on a typical downtown 2-story development
1 acre = 43,560 ft^2
"Property Area" = "Site Area"
Property Density (ft^2/ac) = Building (ft^2)/Site Area (ac)
Density Radius (LF) = 3[Site Area (ft^2)]$^{1/2}$
Density Boundary = Arc of Density Radius (all properties "on or within" the radius are included)
Development Density = Bldgs (ft^2)/Sites (ac) (exclude the Site's parks, waterways, roads, and right-of-ways)

Residential Area: zoned for housing with at least 10 units per acre

Calculations: See above

Exemplary Performance: Meet requirements of Option 1, **AND**

- Property Density at least double the Development Density
- Development Density minimum of <u>120,000 ft^2/ac</u> using a Density Radius at double the Property Area

Design Submittal:
- Option 1: Site vicinity plan with project site and surrounding sites/bldgs; draw Density Boundary or note scale
- Option 1: List of Property/Site Areas and Building Areas on or within Density Boundary

- Option 2: Site vicinity drawing with ½ mile radius and location of Services
- Option 2: List of all Services within ½ mile radius

Environmental Impact: Transportation, Productivity
Economic Impact: Reduces new infrastructure
Community Impact: Urban projects cause more time in cars, need for more cars, erratic and unstable living patterns

Timeline/Team: Site selection process – owner, developer and entire team
Regional Variations: na
O&M Considerations: Provide room for the critical aspects of sustainable operations; maintain air quality

SS Credit 3 Brownfield Development (1, 1, 1)

Intent: Rehabilitate damaged sites where development is complicated by environmental contamination (from hazardous substances, pollutants or contaminants), thereby reducing pressure on undeveloped land.

Requirements:

OPTION 1

Develop on a site <u>documented as contaminated</u> by means of an ASTM E1903-97 Phase II Environmental Site Assessment or a local Voluntary Cleanup Program

OPTION 2

Develop on a site defined as a brownfield by a local, state or federal government agency

<u>Schools can achieve this point only via SS Pr 2: Environmental Site Assessment, and remediating site contamination.</u>

Technology and Strategy:

- Give preference to brownfield sites
- Identify tax incentives and property cost savings
- Coordinate site development plans with remediation activity as appropriate
- Gain community support
- Utilize remediation experts
- Clean site using established techniques

CERCLA (aka "Superfund"): for <u>abandoned or historical</u> waste sites and contamination
RCRA (Resource Conservation and Recovery Act): for active and future facilities "from cradle to grave"

Ex-Situ Remediation: Removal of contaminated soil and groundwater
In-Situ Remediation: Treatment of contaminants in place (injection wells or reactive trenches)

Calculations: na

Exemplary Performance: na

Design Submittal

Environmental Impact: Removes hazardous material from the soil and ground water
Economic Impact: Contributes to social and economic revitalization of bad neighborhoods

Timeline/Team: Site selection process – consult environmental consultant to conduct a site assessment, identify contaminants and schedule remediation with the GC

Regional Variations: Preliminary screening or remediation criteria may vary.

O&M Considerations: Ongoing remediation, monitoring and reporting may be required.

SS Credit 4.1 Alternative Transportation: Public Transportation Access (6, 4, 6)

Intent: Reduce pollution and land development impacts from automobile use.
Requirements:

OPTION 1: Rail Station Proximity

- Locate the project within ½ mile walking distance of an existing - or planned and funded - commuter rail, light rail or subway station (as measured from a main building entrance).

OPTION 2: Bus Stop Proximity

- Within ¼ mile walking distance of 1 or more stops for 2 or more public, campus or private bus lines usable by building occupants (as measured from a main building entrance).
- **Schools: A school bus system may count as 1 of these lines.**

OPTION 3: Pedestrian Access (Schools Only)

- Project must have an attendance boundary such that at least 80% of students live within no more that ¾ mile walking distance for grades 8 and below and 1½ mile walking distance for grades 9 and above.
- Locate the project on a site that allows pedestrian access to the site from all residential neighborhoods that house the planned student population.

ALL OPTIONS:

- Provide dedicated walking or biking lanes to the transit lines that extend from the school building at least to the end of the school property in 2 or more directions without any barriers on school property.

Technology and Strategy:

- Survey the future building occupants to identify transportation needs.
- Build near mass transit.
- Option 3: assess the percentage of the total incoming student population that falls within the specified walking distance radius

Ridership increases by ½% per 1% growth in service

Calculations: na

Exemplary Performance: Option 1 – Comprehensive Transportation Plan: the plan must demonstrate a quantifiable reduction in personal auto use via multiple alternative options; only 1 point is available for SS Credit 4.

Design Submittal

Environmental Impact: Decreased auto emissions, decreased oil extraction/refining, fewer parking spaces.
Economic Impact: Increased value and marketability of the building, decreased parking lot maintenance.

Timeline/Team: Site selection process – architect, design team and client determine the location.

Regional Variations: na

O&M Considerations: Establish a program to inform and reward occupants.

SS Credit 4.2 Alternative Transportation: Bicycle Storage and Changing Rooms (1, 1, 2)

Intent: Reduce pollution and land development impacts from automobile use.
Requirements:

New Construction

CASE 1 – Commercial or Institutional Projects:
- Provide secure bicycle racks and/or storage <u>within 200 yards</u> of an entrance for <u>5% or more</u> of <u>all</u> bldg **peak period users.**
- Provide shower/changing facilities <u>in the building or within 200 yards</u> of an entrance for ½% of **FTE occupants.**

CASE 2 – Residential Projects:
- Provide covered storage facilities for securing bikes for <u>15% or more occupants</u> in lieu of changing/shower facilities.

Schools:

- Provide secure bike racks and/or storage within 200 yards of a building entrance for 5% or more of all **staff and students** above grade level 3 (measured at **peak periods**).
- Provide shower/changing facilities <u>in the building or within 200 yards</u> of an entrance for ½% of <u>FTE</u> **staff.**
- Provide <u>dedicated bike lanes</u> that extend at least to the end of the school property in 2 or more directions without any barriers.

Core & Shell:

CASE 1 – Commercial or Institutional Projects **≤ 300,000 Square Feet**
- Provide secure bicycle racks and/or storage <u>within 200 yards</u> of entrance for <u>3% or more</u> of <u>all</u> bldg **annual average users**.
- Provide shower/changing facilities <u>in the building or within 200 yards</u> of an entrance for ½% of **FTE occupants**.

CASE 2 – Commercial or Institutional Projects **> 300,000 Square Feet**
- Provide secure bicycle racks and/or storage <u>within 200 yards</u> of an entrance for <u>3%</u> of the **occupants** for <u>up to 300,000 sq ft</u> and an additional ½% for the **occupants** for the space <u>over 300,000 sq. ft</u>.
- <u>Mixed use buildings</u> with <u>> 300,000 gross</u> sq ft must <u>apply this calculation for each use of the building</u>.

CASE 3 – Residential Projects:
- Provide covered storage facilities for securing bikes for <u>15% or more occupants</u> in lieu of changing/shower facilities.
- <u>Case 3 must be used by residential buildings or the residential portion</u> of a mixed use building.

Appendix 1:   Default Occupancy Counts (occupancy count requirements and guidance).
FTE Occupants =   full time equivalent occupants = <u>Occupant Hours / 8</u>
Transient Occupants = students, visitors, customers
Peak Occupants =   FTEs + Peak Period Transients

Technology and Strategy:
- Design the building with transportation amenities such as bicycle racks and shower/changing facilities

Calculations: See above

Exemplary Performance: Option 1 – Comprehensive Transportation Plan: the plan must demonstrate a quantifiable reduction in personal auto use via multiple alternative options; <u>only 1 point is available for SS Credit 4</u>.

Design Submittal
Environmental Impact: Decreased auto emissions, decreased oil extraction/refining, fewer parking spaces
Economic Impact: Initial cost for bike storage and shower/changing is low relative to total project cost

Timeline/Team: Bike storage & shower facilities should be in the design concepts during schematic design and design development – architect, plumbing engineer, civil engineer and/or landscape architect.
Regional Variations: Important in areas with good but unrealized potential or no promotion by the city; improves air quality.
O&M Considerations: Establish a program to inform and reward occupants.

SS Credit 4.3 Alternative Transportation: Low-Emitting & Fuel Efficient Vehicles (3, 2, 3)

Intent: Reduce pollution and land development impacts from automobile use.
Requirements:

OPTION 1

New Construction and Core & Shell:

- Provide <u>preferred parking</u> for low-emitting vehicles and fuel-efficient vehicles (FEVs) for <u>5% of total vehicle parking capacity</u> of the site.
- **OR**, <u>discount</u> parking by <u>minimum 20%</u> for <u>all</u> low-emitting vehicles and FEV customers for a <u>min. 2 yrs</u> and <u>post the discount</u> at the parking entrance.
- **<u>C&S:</u> If there are market barriers to the definition of preferred parking, alternatives are considered case by case.**

Schools:

- Provide <u>preferred parking</u> for low-emitting and FEVs for <u>5% of total vehicle parking capacity</u> of the site.
- Provide at least 1 designated carpool drop-off area for low-emitting vehicles and FEVs.

OPTION 2

New Construction and Core & Shell:

- Install <u>alternative-fuel refueling</u> stations for <u>3% of parking capacity</u> (liquid or gaseous stations separately ventilated).

Schools:

- Develop and implement a plan for the busses and maintenance vehicles serving the school to us 20% (by vehicles, fuel or both) natural gas, propane or biodiesel or to be low-emitting vehicles and FEVs.
- Provide at least 1 designated carpool drop-off area for low-emitting vehicles and FEVs.

OPTION 3

New Construction only

- Provide <u>low-emitting vehicles and FEVs</u> for <u>3% of FTE occupants</u>.
- Provide <u>preferred parking</u> for these vehicles.

OPTION 4

New Construction only

- Provide occupants access to a low-emitting/fuel efficient <u>vehicle sharing program</u> according to the following requirements:
  - One low-emitting or FEV must be provided <u>per 3% of FTE</u>, <u>assuming 8 people</u> per vehicle (i.e. 1 vehicle per 267 FTEs); for buildings with <u>less than 267 FTEs</u>, at <u>least 1 vehicle must be provided</u>.
  - A vehicle sharing <u>contract</u> with a term of at least <u>2 years</u> must be provided.
  - <u>Document</u> the estimated number of customers served per vehicle.
  - A <u>narrative</u> explaining program and its administration must be submitted.
  - Low-emitting and FEV parking must be in the <u>nearest spaces</u> in the <u>nearest lot</u>; provide site/area plan clearly highlighting the walking path from the parking to the project site and <u>note the distance</u>.

SS Credit 4.3 (cont.)

Preferred Parking: spaces closest to the main entrance (excluding handicapped) or spaces that are discounted
Low-Emitting Vehicles or FEVs: ZEVs rating by the California Air Resources Board, or a minimum 40 Green Score
by the American Council for an Energy Efficiency Economy (ACEEE)
GHG: Green House Gases
Hybrid: gas engine drives a generator, the generator and/or batteries power electric motors that drive the wheels

Technology and Strategy:

- Provide transportation amenities such as refueling stations.
- Consider sharing the costs and benefits of refueling stations with neighboring buildings.

Calculations: See above; Note: a Hybrid is an alternative fuel vehicle for the purposes of LEED

Exemplary Performance: Option 1 – Comprehensive Transportation Plan: the plan must demonstrate a quantifiable reduction in personal auto use via multiple alternative options; only 1 point is available for SS Credit 4.

Design Submittal

Environmental Impact: Decreased auto emissions, increased air quality, decreased oil extraction/refining.
Economic Impact: Initial cost is high but may be offset by tax incentives.

Timeline/Team: Should be in the design concepts during schematic design and design development – architect, owner, design team.

Regional Variations: Consider the existing infrastructure for alternative fuels.

O&M Considerations: Establish procedures for occupants and staff. Provide special maintenance and safety procedures if alternative fuel stations are used.

SS Credit 4.4 Alternative Transportation: Parking Capacity (2, 2, 2)

Intent: Reduce pollution and land development impacts from <u>single occupancy</u> automobile use.

Requirements:

New Construction and Core & Shell

CASE 1 – Non-Residential Projects

OPTION 1
- Size parking capacity to meet, but not exceed, minimum local zoning requirements.
- **New Construction (additional)**: provide <u>preferred parking</u> for carpools or vanpools for 5% of the total parking spaces.

OPTION 2
- For projects with parking for less than **[5% for NC]** **[3% C&S]** of FTE occupants, provide <u>preferred parking</u> for carpools or vanpools for **[5% for NC]** **[3% C&S]** of the total parking spaces.
- Provide <u>discount</u> parking by <u>minimum 20%</u> for <u>all "poolers"</u> for a <u>min. 2 yrs</u> and <u>post the discount</u> at the parking entrance.

OPTION 3
- Provide no new parking.

CASE 2 – Residential Projects

OPTION 1
- Size parking capacity to meet, but not exceed, minimum local zoning requirements.
- Provide infrastructure and support programs to facilitate shared vehicle usage.

OPTION 2
- Provide no new parking.

CASE 3 – Mixed Use (Residential with Commercial/Retail) Projects

OPTION 1
- For mixed with < 10% commercial area, consider the entire building residential and use Case 2.
- For mixed with > 10% commercial area, commercial goes by Case 1 and residential goes by Case 2.

OPTION 2
- Provide no new parking.

All Cases: C&S only - See Appendix 1 – Default Occupancy Counts for occupancy count requirements and guidance.

Schools

OPTION 1
- Size parking capacity to meet, but not exceed, minimum local zoning requirements.
- Provide <u>preferred parking</u> for carpools or vanpools for 5% of the total parking spaces.

OPTION 2
- Provide no new parking.

OPTION 3
- For projects that have no minimum local zoning requirements, provide 25% fewer parking spaces than the applicable standard listed in the 2003 Institute of Transportation Engineers (ITE) "Parking Generation" study.

Technology and Strategy:

- Minimize parking lot/garage size. Consider sharing parking facilities with adjacent buildings.
- Consider alternatives that will limit the use of single occupancy vehicles.

Calculations: See above

Exemplary Performance: Option 1 – Comprehensive Transportation Plan: the plan must demonstrate a quantifiable reduction in personal auto use via multiple alternative options; only 1 point is available for SS Credit 4.

Design Submittal:

- Case 1, Opt 1: FTEs and total parking capacity; provide local code requirements, provide the # of "pooler" spaces on site
- Case 1, Opt 2: FTEs and total parking capacity; provide the number of "pooler" spaces marked as such
- Case 2, Opt 1: FTEs and total parking capacity; describe the infrastructure/programs to support and promote pooling
- All Cases/Options for no new parking: FTEs and total parking capacity
- Case 3: If < 10% commercial use Case 2, Opt 1; if > 10% commercial, commercial uses Case 1 and residential uses Case 2.

Environmental Impact: Saves energy, reduces impact, less asphalt

Economic Impact: More occupants, less land to buy and maintain

Timeline/Team: Discuss during concept phase and incorporate during schematic design and design development.

Regional Variations: na

O&M Considerations: Establish procedures for occupants and staff, e.g. enforcement, discounts, tracking.

SS Credit 5.1 Site Development: Protect or Restore Habitat (1, 1, 1)

Intent: Conserve existing natural areas and restore damaged areas to provide habitat and promote biodiversity.

Requirements:

CASE 1 – Greenfield Sites

Limit all site disturbances as follows:
- 40 feet beyond the building perimeter
- 10 feet beyond surface walkways, patios, surface parking and utilities less than 12" in diameter
- 15 feet beyond primary roadway curbs and main utility branch trenches
- 25 feet beyond constructed areas with permeable surfaces (pervious paving, stormwater detention facilities, playing fields) that require additional staging areas in order to limit compaction in the constructed areas

CASE 2 – Previously Developed Areas or Graded Sites

- Restore or protect a minimum of 50% of the site area (excluding the building footprint) with native or adapted vegetation or 20% of the total site area (including the building footprint), whichever is greater.
- Vegetated roof can apply to the calculation if the project earns SS Cr2 (Density) and the plants are native/adapted and provide the habitat and biodiversity intent of the credit.

Greenfield Site: not previously developed or graded and remains in a natural state
Previously Developed Site: previously contained buildings, roadways, parking lots or were graded or altered by humans

Native Plants: indigenous to a locality and are not considered invasive species or noxious weeds; require minimal or no irrigation, maintenance or chemicals; provide habitat value & promote biodiversity through <u>avoiding monoculture planting</u>
Adapted Plants: cultivars of native plants that are adapted to the local climate and not considered invasive or noxious

Technology and Strategy:

Greenfield Sites:
- Perform site survey to identify site elements and adopt a master plan for development of the site.
- Site the building to minimize the disruption to ecosystems and design the building to minimize the footprint.
- Establish clearly marked construction boundaries to minimize disturbance and restore degraded areas.

Previously Developed Sites:
- Utilize local/regional agencies, consultants, educational facilities and native plant societies as <u>resources for selection</u>.
- Prohibit plant materials listed as invasive or noxious weed species.

Calculations: See above

Exemplary Performance: Restore or protect a minimum of 75% of the site area (excluding the building footprint), or 30% of the total site (including building footprint), whichever is greater, with native or adapted vegetation.

Construction Submittal

Environmental Impact: Prevent/reduce ecological site damage; site restoration
Economic Impact: Native and/or adapted plants require lower maintenance

CIVIL ENGINEER

Timeline/Team: Site Design – minimize footprint and impervious areas, identify important environmental characteristics, identify construction entrances and setbacks: landscape architects, ecologists, environ engineers, civil engineers, government officials.

Regional Variations: Focus on protecting/resoring vegetation and ecological features appropriate to the local area.
O&M Considerations: Minimize hardscape maintenance, allergens and pest attracters; establish a sustainable landscape management plan; water and weed for the first 2 or 3 years.

SS Credit 5.2 Site Development: Maximize Open Space (1, 1, 1)

Intent: Provide a high ratio of open space to development footprint to promote biodiversity.

Requirements:

CASE 1 – Sites with Local Zoning Open Space Requirements

Reduce the development footprint and/or provide vegetated open space within the project boundary to <u>exceed</u> the local zoning's open space requirement for the site <u>by 25%</u>.

CASE 2 – Sites with No Local Zoning Requirements (e.g. some universities, military bases)

Provide vegetated open space adjacent to the building <u>equal to its footprint</u>.

CASE 3 – Sites with Zoning Ordinances but No Open Space Requirements

Provide vegetated open space <u>equal to 20%</u> of the site area.

ALL CASES:

- For projects in urban areas that earn SS Cr2 (Density), vegetated roof areas can contribute to credit compliance.
- For projects in urban areas that earn SS Cr2 (Density), pedestrian oriented hardscape areas can contribute to credit compliance if a minimum of 25% of the open space counted is vegetated.

Development Footprint: total area of the building footprint, hardscape, access roads and parking
Green Roofs: plants, growth medium, filter cloth, drainage, water and root repellant membrane, support structure
Open Space: as defined by local zoning, or [Property Area – Development Footprint] in absence of local zoning, and vegetated and pervious; **wetlands and natural ponds are part of the open space if vegetated and the gradient is $\leq$ 1:4**.

Technology and Strategy:

- Perform site survey to identify site elements and adopt a master plan for development of the site.
- Select a suitable building location and design the building to minimize the footprint and minimize site disruption
- Try stacking the building program, tuck-under parking and sharing facilities with neighbors to maximize open space.

Calculations: See above

Exemplary Performance:

- Case 1: Exceed local zoning requirements for vegetated open space by 50%.
- Case 2: Provide vegetated open space adjacent to building equal to twice the building footprint.
- Case 3: Provide vegetated open space equal to 40% of project site area.

Design Submittal:

- Case 1: Site and footprint areas, drawings highlighting vegetated open space; area required and area provided.
- Case 2: Site and footprint areas, drawings highlighting vegetated open space; area provided.
- Case 3: Site and footprint areas, drawings highlighting vegetated open space; area provided.

Environmental Impact: Provide habitat for vegetation

Economic Impact: Preservation reduces landscaping costs

Timeline/Team: Site Selection and Design Phase – minimize footprint, identify important environmental characteristics, identify construction entrances and setbacks: landscape architects, civil engineers, government officials.

Regional Variations: na
O&M Considerations: For native/adapted vegetation, see Cr 5.1; for monoculture or non-native plants, choose species with low water, fertilizer and maintenance requirements; minimize hardscape maintenance, allergens and pest attracters.

SS Credit 6.1 Stormwater Design: Quantity Control (1, 1, 1)

Intent: Limit disruption of natural water hydrology by reducing impervious cover, increasing on-site infiltration, reducing or eliminating pollution from stormwater runoff, and eliminating contaminants.

Requirements:

CASE 1 – Sites with Existing Imperviousness 50% or Less

Option 1: Implement a stormwater management plan that prevents the post-construction peak discharge rate and quantity from exceeding the pre-construction peak discharge rate and quantity for the one- and two-year 24-hour design storms.

Option 2: Implement a stormwater management plan that **protects receiving stream channels** from excessive erosion by implementing a stream channel protection strategy and quantity control strategies.

CASE 2 – Sites with Existing Imperviousness Greater than 50%

- Implement a stormwater management plan that results in a 25% decrease in the volume of stormwater runoff from the 2-year 24-hour design storm.

Bioswale:	swaled course, removes silt and pollution from runoff, side slopes < 6%
Vr:	volume of runoff
Rv:	runoff coefficient
I:	imperviousness

Technology and Strategy:

- **Minimize Impervious Area**: reduce building footprint, pervious paving, Green Roof, bioswales/vegetative filter strips, retention ponds, cluster developments.
- Minimize runoff through infiltration, reuse runoff for non-potable water.
- Harvesting considerations:
    - Amount needed for intended use
    - Draw-down between storms
    - Drainage area and % that is impervious (i.e. availability)
    - Conveyance system (should be clearly marked)
    - Pretreatment (e.g. screens, filters)
    - Pressure of stored water is at 0.43 psi/ft (irrigation needs 15 psi)
    - Trade-off: more pervious surface limits loads, need additional area, Green Roof reduces Harvesting
    - Synergy: underground parking reduces runoff and reduces heat island

Calculations:
Volume (runoff captured via collection facilities): $V_r(ft^3) = P \times R_v \times A / 12"$, where **P** = avg rainfall event (in.),
$R_v = 0.05 + 0.009 \times I$ (I = % imperviousness of the collection surface), **A** = area of collection surface (ft^2)
Minimum Drawdown Rate: $Q_r(ft^3/sec) = $ **Tank Capacity (ft^3) / Rainfall Event Interval (sec)**

Exemplary Performance: Document a comprehensive approach to capture and treat stormwater runoff and demonstrate performance above and beyond the credit requirements (**only 1 ID point for either SS 6.1 or SS 6.2**).

Design Submittal

Environmental Impact: Limits loss of capacity to prevent runoff and absorb rain, and limits "Bankfull" events
Economic Impact: Adding natural drainage systems early in site planning keeps costs down, helps municipal govts

Timeline/Team: Design during earliest planning stages and integrate with landscape and building plans; CIVIL ENGINEER, landscape architect.

Regional Variations: Dramatic variation across climate zones; great for generally dry regions with seasonally heavy rainfall.

O&M Considerations: Ongoing inspection and maintenance plan; at a minimum, include periodic visual inspections and recommendations.

SS Credit 6.2 Stormwater Design: Quality Control (1, 1, 1)

Intent: Limit disruption and pollution of natural water flows by managing stormwater runoff

Requirements:

Implement stormwater management plan that:

- reduces impervious cover (perviousness < 50% and promotes runoff)
- promotes infiltration
- **captures and treats stormwater runoff from 90%** of the average rainfall event using acceptable **BMPs**, i.e.
  - Humid Watersheds: 1" of rainfall per average rainfall event
  - Semi-arid Watersheds: ¾" of rainfall per average rainfall event
  - Arid Watersheds: ½" of rainfall per average rainfall event
- Data must conform to accepted protocol for BMP monitoring, e.g. Technology Acceptance Reciprocity Partnership.
- BMPs used to treat runoff must be **capable of removing 80%** of the average annual post-construction **TSS** load based on existing monitoring reports. BMPs are considered to meet these criteria if:
  Opt 1: They are designed in accordance with standards and specifications from a state/local program with the above criteria.
  Opt 2: There exist in-field performance monitoring data demonstrating compliance with the criteria; data must conform to accepted protocol for BMP monitoring, e.g. Technology Acceptance Reciprocity Partnership.

BMP:	Best Management Practice
TSS:	Total Suspended Solids
Alternative Surfaces:	vegetated roofs, pervious pavement, grid pavers
Structural Techniques:	cisterns, manholes, ponds, sewer repair/combination
Non-Structural Techniques:	rain gardens, vegetated swales, disconnection of imperviousness, rainwater recycling
Sustainable Designs:	Low Impact Development, Environmentally Sensitive Design
Humid Watershed Climate:	40" or more of rainfall each year, 1" runoff per average rainfall event
Semi-arid Watershed Climate:	20" to 40" of rainfall each year, ¾" of rainfall per average rainfall event
Arid Watershed Climate:	less than 20" of rainfall each year, ½" of rainfall per average rainfall event

Technology and Strategy:

- **Minimize Impervious Area**: use alternative surfaces and non-structural techniques to reduce imperviousness and promote infiltration, thereby reducing pollutant loadings.
- Treat stormwater runoff: use sustainable design strategies to design integrated natural and mechanical systems such as constructed wetlands, vegetated filters and open channels.

Calculations: Depends on available data and the preference of the CIVIL ENGINEER, but must be widely accepted and recognized.

Exemplary Performance: Document a comprehensive approach to capture and treat stormwater runoff and demonstrate performance above and beyond the credit requirements (**only 1 ID point for either SS 6.1 or SS 6.2**).

Design Submittal

Environmental Impact:	Reduces sedimentation and pollution
Economic Impact:	Reduces municipal infrastructure for conveyance and treatment of stormwater

Timeline/Team: Pre-design – owner, architect, engineers; Schematic Design – Civil Engineer, Mechanical Engineer, Landscape Architect; Design Development – Civil Engineer or Landscape Architect; Construction Documents – Civil Engineer, Landscape Architect, Architect, Owner.

Regional Variations: Consider the watershed where project is to be located and the amount of rainfall on the project site. BMPs must be specific to the site and appropriate to the region.

O&M Considerations: Ongoing inspection and maintenance plan; at a minimum, include periodic visual inspections and recommendations. Pervious systems require ongoing maintenance; structural measures usually require more maintenance.

SS Credit 7.1 Heat Island Effect: Non-Roof (1, 1, 1)

Intent: Reduce heat islands to minimize the impact on the microclimate and the human and wildlife habitat.

Requirements:

OPTION 1

Use any combo of the following strategies for **50% of the site hardscape** (roads, sidewalks, courtyards, parking lots)

- Provide shade from existing tree canopy or within 5 years of installation, trees in place by time of occupancy.
- Provide shade from structures fully covered by solar PV panels that offset some non-renewable resource use.
- Provide shade from architectural devices or structures that have an SRI of at least 29.
- Have hardscape materials with an SRI of at least 29.
- Have an open-grid pavement system that is at least 50% pervious.

OPTION 2

Place a minimum of **50% of parking spaces under cover** (under ground, deck, roof or building). If under a roof, the roof must have an SRI of at least 29 and be either a vegetated green roof or covered by PV panels that offset non-renewable energy use.

Heat Island:	thermal gradient difference between developed and undeveloped areas
Shade:	calculated on June 21 at noon solar time
SRI:	Solar Reflectance Index, measure of ability to reject solar heat (from 0 for black to 100 for white)
Albedo:	Reflectance
Reflectance:	ratio of reflected solar energy to the incoming solar energy (from 0 to 1 or 0% to 100%)
Emmitance:	ability to shed infrared radiation (from 0 to 1 or 0% to 100%), a shiny metal surface has low emmitance
Emmisivity:	ratio of emitted radiation to the emitted radiation from a block body at the same temperature

Technology and Strategy:

- **Minimize Heat Absorption by Exterior Materials**: use strategies, materials, landscaping.
- Use shade from native or adapted trees and large shrubs, vegetated trellises, or other structures supporting vegetation.
- Use new coatings and integral colorants for asphalt to achieve light-colored surfaces instead of blacktop.
- Position PV cells to shade impervious surfaces.
- Consider replacing constructed surfaces with vegetated surfaces and open grid paving or with high albedo materials.

Calculations:
- T = sum of the areas of the non-roof hardscape surfaces on the project site
- O = sum of the areas of the hardscape surfaces with an open grid paving system that are minimum 50% pervious
- R = sum of the areas of the hardscape features that have an SRI of at least 29
- S = effective shaded area = arithmetic mean of the total shade from hardscape features at 10,12 & 3 on June 21
- E = sum of all the areas of the hardscape surfaces shaded by solar energy panels
- A = sum of all the areas of the hardscape surfaces shaded by architectural devices or structures with SRI at least 29
- Q = Qualifying Area = S + E + A + R + O, must be $\geq$ 50% of T

Exemplary Performance: 100% for Options 1 and 2

Construction Submittal
Environmental Impact: Preservation and restoration of cooling and evapotranspiration

Economic Impact: Reduced cooling costs and energy consumption

Timeline/Team: Design – Landscape Architect, Architect, Civil Engineer; Construction Documents – specify materials with low emissivity or high SRI.

Regional Variations: Heat island intensity depends on weather/climate, proximity to water bodies and topography.
O&M Considerations: Clean materials with high reflectivity every 2 years. Maintain open-grip pavement. Care for and maintain trees and vegetation to ensure anticipated shading within five years.

SS Credit 7.2 Heat Island Effect: Roof (1, 1, 1)

Intent: Reduce heat islands to minimize the impact on the microclimate and the human and wildlife habitat.

Requirements:

OPTION 1

- Use roofing materials with an **SRI ≥ 78 for low-sloped and ≥ 29 for steep-sloped** on a minimum of **75%** of roof surface.
- If more than 75% is covered, the SRI can be less because a weighted average is used to get an equivalent SRI for 75%.

OPTION 2

- Install a vegetated roof for at least **50%** of the roof area (vegetation, growing medium, filter fabric, drainage, water-proof membrane, roof structure); one negative is that a vegetated roof may cause bird collisions.

OPTION 3

- Install high albedo (reflectance) and vegetated roof surfaces that, in combination, meet the following:

$$\text{(Area of SRI Roof / 0.75)} + \text{(Area of Vegetated Roof / 0.5)} \geq \text{Total Roof Area}$$

Low-slope:	slope ≤ 2:12	SRI = 78
Steep-slope:	slope > 2:12	SRI = 29

Heat Island:	thermal gradient difference between developed and undeveloped areas
SRI:	Solar Reflectance Index: measure of ability to reject solar heat (from 0 for black to 100 for white)
Albedo:	Reflectance
Reflectance:	ratio of reflected solar energy to the incoming solar energy (from 0 to 1 or 0% to 100%)
Emmitance:	ability to shed infrared radiation (from 0 to 1 or 0% to 100%), shiny metal surface has low emmitance
Emmisivity:	ratio of emitted radiation to the emitted radiation from a block body at the same temperature
ASTM:	American Society for Testing & Materials

Technology and Strategy:

- **Minimize Heat Absorption by Exterior Materials**: Use high-Albedo, high-emmisivity and vegetated roofs

Calculations:
- T = sum of the areas of the non-roof hardscape surfaces on the project site
- O = sum of the areas of the hardscape surfaces with an open grid paving system that are min 50% pervious
- R = sum of the areas of the hardscape features that have an SRI of at least 29
- S = effective shaded area = arithmetic mean of total shade from hardscape features at 10,12 & 3 on June 21
- Q = Qualifying Area = O + R + S, must be ≥ 50% of T

Exemplary Performance: 100% Green Roof excluding mechanical rooms, PV panels and skylights

Design Submittal

Environmental Impact:	Reduces roof temperature; Green Roofs reduce run-off
Economic Impact:	Reduced cooling costs and energy consumption

Timeline/Team: Early Design Phase – Landscape Architect, Architect, Civil Engineer; Mechanical Engineer, Ecologist; Construction Documents – Architect, Contractor.

Regional Variations: Buildings in urban areas and climate zones 1, 2 and 3 are most affected by heat islands. Consider weather/climate, proximity to water bodies and topography.

O&M Considerations: Clean materials with high reflectivity every 2 years. Select plantings that are easy to maintain and without airborne seeds. Inspect periodically. Maintain drainage paths. Design for mowing and cutting.

SS Credit 8 Light Pollution Reduction (1, 1, 1)

Intent: Minimize light trespass from the building and site, reduce sky-glow to increase night sky access, improve nighttime visibility through glare reduction, and reduce development impact on nocturnal environments.

Requirements:

INTERIOR LIGHTING

Option 1

- All non-emergency interior fixtures with direct line of sight to any openings in the envelope (translucent or transparent) shall have input **power reduced** (by automatic device) by at least **50% between 11 pm and 5 am**.
- After-hours override may be provided (manual or occupant sensor), the override to last a maximum of 30 minutes.

Option 2

- All openings in the envelope (translucent or transparent) with a direct line of sight to any non-emergency luminaires shall have **shielding** (resultant T_{vis} < 10%) that will be **controlled/closed** by automatic device **between 11 pm and 5 am**.

EXTERIOR LIGHTING [**LZ2 = 200-3,000 people/sq.mi, LZ3 = over 3,000 people/sq.mi, LZ4 = 100,000 people/sq.mi**]

- Only light areas as required for safety/comfort; <u>Lighting Power Densities</u> not to exceed 90.1-2007 (with errata but without addenda) for the zone classification.
- Exterior lighting control requirements from 90.1-2007, Exterior Lighting Section without amendments (with errata but without addenda).

All projects shall be classified as one of the following zones per IESNA RP-33, and shall follow all zone requirements.

LZ1: Dark (Developed areas within national parks, state parks, forest land and rural areas)
- Site & bldg-mounted with max initial illumin < 0.01 fc horizontal/vertical at and beyond the site boundary
- Document that 0% of the sum total initial design fixture lumens are emitted at an angle > 90 degrees from nadir

LZ2: Low (Areas predominantly Residential, Neighborhood Bus. Districts, Light Indus w limited night use, Mixed Resid.)
- Site & bldg-mounted with max initial illumin < 0.1fc horizontal/vertical at the boundary, < 0.01fc horiz 10' beyond
- Document that < 2% of the sum total initial design fixture lumens are emitted at an angle > 90 degrees from nadir
- If site boundary abuts public rights-of-way, light trespass requirements may be met using curb line as boundary

LZ3: Medium (All other areas not included in LZ1, LZ2 or LZ4 such as Commercial/Industrial or High-density Residential)
- Site & bldg-mounted with max initial illumin < 0.2 fc horizontal/vertical at the boundary, < 0.01fc horiz 15' beyond
- Document that < 5% of the sum total initial design fixture lumens are emitted at an angle > 90 degrees from nadir
- If site boundary abuts public rights-of-way, light trespass requirements may be met using curb line as boundary

LZ4: High (High activity commercial district in major metro areas; **must be designated LZ4 by local jurisdiction**)
- Site & bldg-mounted with max initial illumin < 0.6 fc horizontal/vertical at the boundary, < 0.01fc horiz 15' beyond
- Document that < 10% of the sum total initial design fixt. lumens are emitted at an angle > 90 degrees from nadir
- If site boundary abuts public rights-of-way, light trespass requirements may be met using curb line as boundary

All: For a single light at the intersection of private driveway and public road, use centerline of road for 2x driveway width

Footcandle: 1 lumen/ft^2 from a one candela light source at a distance of 1 foot (additive for multiple sources on same surface).
Candela: luminous intensity
Nadir: straight down
LPD: Light Power Density
IESNA: Illuminating Engineering Society of North America

Technology and Strategy:

- Avoid off-site lighting and night sky pollution through <u>use of a computer model</u>.
- Use full cutoff lights, low-reflectance surfaces, low-angle spotlights.
- Address site Illuminance Level, Luminaire Distribution, pre-curfew (before 10 pm or at business closing) & post-curfew.
- Hire a professional.
- Review ordinances and bylaws.
- Determine the environmental Zone.
- Use least possible lighting for adequate glare.
- Select lights with good lighting and reduced maintenance costs.
- Design for minimum upward illumination from reflection.
- Use minimum lighting required and only on required areas.
- Commission following construction.

Project teams wishing to use addenda approved by ASHRAE for the purposes of this credit may do so, but addenda must be applied consistently across all LEED credits.

Calculations:

INTERIOR LIGHTING

- Find direction of maximum luminous intensity (horizontal and vertical candelas) from manufacturer's photometric data.
- Trace this vector from the light to see if it reaches the exterior.

EXTERIOR LIGHTING POWER DENSITY

- Parking, walkways, plazas, etc. W/ft^2
- Façade and landscape W/ft^2

EXTERIOR SKYGLOW and LIGHT TREPASS

- Create "Illumination Model" using lighting design software.
- Create "Calculation Grid" with maximum 10' x 10' squares.
- Use manufacturer's data to determine initial lamp lumens; from photometric data determine same at 90 deg from the nadir.
- Light Trespass: Obtrusive light that is unwanted due to qualitative, directional or spectral attributes.
- Sky Glow: Caused by stray light from unshielded light sources or reflected light that enters the atmosphere and illuminates and reflects off dust, debris and water vapor.

Exemplary Performance: na

Design Submittal

Environmental Impact:	Reduce light pollution and the effect on nocturnal ecosystem
Economic Impact:	Careful design reduces infrastructure and energy costs
Community Impact:	Aesthetics, safety, security, non-intrusive

Timeline/Team: Schematic Design Phase – Lighting designer determines the environmental zone; Design Phase – Photometric analysis is performed; Construction Documents – Landscape Architect, Civil Engineer, lighting designer, Architect, Electric Engineer, all verify layout and compliance.

Regional Variations: na

O&M Considerations: Clean and re-lamp periodically. Group re-lamp if the labor cost exceeds the lamp cost.

SS Credit 9 Tenant design and Construction Guidelines (0, 0, 1)

Intent (for C&S only): To educate tenants about implementing sustainable design and construction features in their tenant improvement build-out. Tenant design and construction guidelines benefit the C&S certified project in 2 important ways:

1. The guidelines will help tenants design and build sustainable interiors and adopt green building practices.
2. The guidelines will help in coordinating LEED 2009 for CI and LEED 2009 for C&S Development certifications.

Requirements:
Publish an illustrated document that provides tenants with the following design and construction information:

- Description of sustainable design and construction features incorporated in the C&S project and the project's sustainability goals and objectives, including those for tenant spaces.
- Information on LEED for CI and how the LEED for C&S credits will contribute to achieving LEED for CI credits.
- Information that enables a tenant to coordinate space design and construction with the C&S's building systems. Specific LEED 2009 for CI credits to be addressed, when applicable, include the following:

Water use reduction	Ventilation and outdoor air delivery
Optimize energy performance, lighting power	Construction indoor air quality management
Optimize energy performance, lighting controls	Indoor chemical and pollutant source control
Optimize energy performance, HVAC	Controllability of systems
Energy use and metering	Thermal comfort
M & V	Daylighting and views
Commissioning	

- Recommendations, including examples, for sustainable strategies, products, materials and services.

Technology and Strategy:
- Tenant guidelines educate the future building tenants on C&S project goals, explain how tenants can incorporate green build-out of their own spaces, describe synergies between C&S and CI, and encourage tenants to pursue CI.
- Recommendations in the tenant guidelines highlight building-specific best practices and are not design requirements.
- **Tenant guidelines must include the following**:
    - **C&S Sustainable Design and Construction Features:** to help tenant design team understand and efficiently utilize the base building's systems and design features.
    - **Information regarding the LEED for Commercial Interiors Rating System:** to help the tenant pursue LEED for CI.

Calculations: na
Exemplary Performance: na
Design Submittal: LEED Online; Retain a copy of the tenant design and construction guidelines.
Environmental Impact:
- Due to the speculative nature of the real estate market, C&S and interior tenant spaces are controlled by different entities.
- Responsibility for environmental impact is weighted differently for owners, developers and tenants.
- Tenant lighting design and daylighting strategies depend on C&S construction.
- Base building mechanical systems will directly influence tenants' ability to optimize occupants' indoor environmental quality.
- LEED for C&S offers tenants environmental benefits built into the project and can inspire tenants to take their own steps.
- Energy and water use reduction measures are important when tenants are required to meter and pay their own utility bills.

Economic Impact:
- Producing tenant guidelines will not have an economic impact on LEED for C&S projects.
- The strategies and recommendation in the guidelines can require upfront investments on the part of building tenants if the tenants choose to certify their build-out projects under LEED for CI.
- Carefully designed C&S developments support cost-effective ways for tenants to earn credits under LEED for CI.

Timeline/Team: Design Phase – Architect, Design Team, Owner; **the document** is part of the design submittal, should be made available to tenants as part of lease negotiations and **must be provided prior to start of any tenant design work.**
Regional Variations: na
O&M Considerations: Guidelines are useful over the building life; consider EBO&M; consider tenant and whole bldg optimization.

SS Credit 9 Site Master Plan (0, 1, 0)

Intent (for Schools only): To ensure that the environmental site issues included in the initial development of the site and project are continued throughout future development caused by changes in programs or demography.

Requirements:

- The project must achieve at least 4 out of the following 7 credits; those 4 credits must then be recalculated using the data from the master plan:

SS Cr 1:	Site Selection
SS Cr 5.1:	Site Development – Protect or Restore Habitat
SS Cr 5.2:	Site Development – Maximize Open Space
SS Cr 6.1:	Stormwater Design – Quantity Control
SS Cr 6.2:	Stormwater Design – Quality Control
SS Cr 7.1:	Heat Island Effect – Nonroof
SS Cr 8:	Light Pollution Reduction

- A site master plan for the school must be developed in collaboration with the school board or other decision-making body.
- Previous sustainable site design measures should be considered, with intent to retain existing infrastructure if possible.
- The master plan must include current and future construction (within the building's lifespan) that affects the site.
- The master plan development footprint must also include parking, paving and utilities.

Technology and Strategy:

- Include plans for community centers, fields, libraries, parks, wetlands, and other major projects that affect community needs.
- There is potential overlap with SS Cr 10: Joint Use of Facilities.
- Involve the local municipality and county.
- Build in flexibility to accommodate a range of scenarios, e.g. reduction in enrollment.

Calculations: See **Requirements**.

Exemplary Performance: na

Design Submittal: LEED Online; Description of the plan's development process in collaboration with the school board or other decision-making body; Retain a copy of the site's master plan and written verification of its approval.

Environmental Impact:
- Expansion of school facilities is often required to accommodate a school's changing needs.
- The master plan ensures that goals remain a priority in future expansion projects.
- The plan helps prevent implementation of "quick fix" solutions that overlook long-term performance and environmental concerns.

Economic Impact:
- A well-developed master plan could help secure future funding by establishing credibility with stakeholders.
- The plan may propose that elements be built into the project in advance of their intended use. This may raise initial costs but will increase efficiency and reduce costs in the future.
- The plan should propose strategies to **accommodate both increasing and decreasing enrollments**.

Timeline/Team: Discussions should take place well in advance of the Predesign Phase to identify environmental and financial impacts – Architect, Owner and Design Team; allow public input from residents, businesses and other neighbors.

Regional Variations: na

O&M Considerations: Use the plan as a required reference for future site alterations; update the plan every 2 to 5 years; make the plan accessible to all stakeholders; designate a party responsible for overseeing the plan's implementation (school administrators are the best option).

SS Credit 10 Joint Use of Facilities (0, 1, 0)

Intent (for Schools only): To make the school a more integrated part of the community by enabling the building and its playing fields to be used for nonschool events and functions.

Requirements:

OPTION 1
- In collaboration with the school board or other decision-making body, ensure that **at least 3 of the following spaces** included in the school are accessible to and available for shared use by the general public: **auditorium, gym, cafeteria/cafetorium, classroom(s), playing fields and/or joint parking**.
- Provide a **separate entry** to the spaces **from a school <u>lobby or corridor near an entrance convenient to public access, which can be secured from the rest of the school after normal school hours and has toilets available</u>**.

OPTION 2
- In collaboration with the school board or other decision-making body, engage in a contract with community or other organizations to provide **at least 2 dedicated-use spaces** in the building. The spaces include, but are not limited to:

Commercial office	Police offices
Health clinic	Library or media center
Parking lot	One or more commercial sector businesses
Community service centers	

- Provide a **separate entry** to the spaces **from a school <u>lobby or corridor near an entrance convenient to public access, which can be secured from the rest of the school after normal school hours and has toilets available</u>**.

OPTION 3
- In collaboration with the school board or other decision-making body, ensure that **at least 2 of the following 6 spaces** that are owned by other organizations/agencies are accessible to students: **auditorium, gym, cafeteria, classroom(s), swimming pool and playing field**.
- Provide direct pedestrian access to these spaces from the school.
- Provide signed agreements with other organizations or agencies that stipulate how they and the school district and organizations or agencies will share these spaces.

Technology and Strategy:

- Agreements are most effective when contact with the community is initiated early, e.g. before property purchases.
- Schools and organizations may pool resources to purchase property.
- Security must be addressed; schools should use caution when engaging organizations and services.

Calculations: na

Exemplary Performance: <u>Meet the requirements of 2 of the 3 Options.</u>

Design Submittal: LEED Online; list the shared spaces; show doors/gates/restrooms; retain documentation.

Environmental Impact:
- Joint-use reduces the need to build on previously undeveloped land, reduces extraction/manufacturing/transportation, reduces amount of paving/runoff/heat island, and may add access or greater proximity to otherwise inaccessible services.

Economic Impact:
- Joint-use can reduce overcrowding, divide the cost of land/construction, and ongoing O&M costs.
- Schools may be able to trade community access for landscaping, snow removal or garbage/recycling services.
- Schools may have to absorb costs for higher safety standards and separate utility metering.

Timeline/Team: There are opportunities to achieve agreements throughout the planning, design and operation of a school; involve city managers, town authorities, school board members, PTA leaders, principals and community members.

Regional Variations: na

O&M Considerations: Agreements should explicitly outline shared costs and responsibilities; address master plan updates.

Water Efficiency (WE) NC 6-10 Pts, Schools 7-11 Pts, C&S 6-10 Pts

- Between 1990 and 2000, public water consumption increased 12% to 43.3 billion gallons per day.
- In 2000, total water use was 48% for thermoelectric power, 34% for irrigation, 11% for public supply and 6% for other uses.
- In 2000, building uses represented slightly less than 40% of the total groundwater withdrawals.
- 86% of withdrawn water is used, treated and discharged to the nation's water bodies.
- 1/3 of lakes, streams and rivers are unsafe for swimming and fishing, but, water bodies are 50% cleaner than in the mid 70s.

- WE prereqs and credits encourage strategies/technologies that reduce the amount of potable water consumed by buildings.
- Many strategies are no-cost or provide a rapid payback.
- Biological wastewater treatment systems and graywater plumbing systems are cost-effective only under certain conditions.

Monitor Water Consumption Performance
- The first step to improving water efficiency is tracking water use alongside energy use.

Reduce Indoor Potable Water Consumption
- Use alternative water sources for nonpotable applications.
- Install new fixtures, flow restrictors on existing fixtures, electronic controls, composting toilets and waterless urinals.

Reduce Water Consumption to Save Energy and Improve Environmental Well-Being
- Water efficiency reduces the amount of energy required for treating, heating, cooling and distributing water.
- Water heating in commercial buildings accounts for nearly 15% of total building energy use.
- 36 states anticipate local, regional or statewide water shortages by 2013.
- Human health and environmental welfare are affected when reservoirs and groundwater aquifers are depleted.
- Water efficiency reduces energy consumption by water treatment/supply facilities, which currently consume 56 billion kWh/yr.

Practice Water-Efficient Landscaping
- Outdoor use of potable water (primarily landscaping) accounts for 30% of the 26 billion gallons consumed daily.
- Maintaining or reestablishing native plants on building sites fosters a self-sustaining landscape.
- Native plants require less water and tend to require less fertilizer and pesticides.

In Schools, Use Water-Efficient Processes as a Teaching Tool
- Educational opportunities include the study of biological systems, nutrient cycles, habitats and the impact of human systems on local watersheds and natural resources.
- Students can calculate their own water use savings while practicing math and environmental stewardship at same time.

WE Prerequisite 1 Water Use Reduction

Intent: Increase water efficiency within buildings to reduce the burden on municipal water supply and wastewater systems.

Requirements:

- Employ strategies that in aggregate use **20% less** water than the water use baseline calculated for the building (NOT INCLUDING IRRIGATION).

The <u>baseline</u> shall meet the requirements of:

- Energy Policy Act of 1992 and subsequent rulings by the Dept of Energy
- Energy Policy Act of 2005
- Fixture performance as stated in the 2006 Editions of the Uniform Plumbing Code or International Plumbing Code

Calculations are based on estimated occupant usage and shall include only the following fixtures and fixture fittings:

- water closets
- urinals
- lavatory faucets
- showers
- kitchen sink faucets
- pre-rinse spray valves

National Efficiency Baselines for Commercial Water-Using Fixtures, Fittings and Appliances

Fixtures, Fittings and Appliances	Current Baseline
Commercial Toilets	1.6 gpf* except blow-out fixtures: 3.5 gpf
Commercial Urinals	1.0 gpf
Commercial Lavatory (restroom) Faucets	2.2 gpm at 60 psi – private applications only (hotel/motel guest rooms, hospital patient rooms) 0.5 gpm at 60 psi** – all others except private applications 0.25 gallons per cycle for metering faucets
Commercial Pre-rinse Spray Valves (for food service applications)	Flow rate $\leq$ 1.6 gpm (no pressure specified; no performance requirement)

National Efficiency Baselines for Residential Water-Using Fixtures, Fittings and Appliances

Fixtures, Fittings and Appliances	Current Baseline
Residential Toilets	1.6 gpf***
Residential Lavatory (Bathroom) Faucets	2.2 gpm at 60 psi
Residential Kitchen Faucet	
Residential Showerheads	2.5 gpm at 80 psi per shower stall****

*EPAct 1992 standard for toilets applies to both commercial and residential models
**In addition to EPAct requirements, ASME standard for public lavatory faucets is 0.5 gpm at 60 psi. This maximum has been incorporated into the national Uniform Plumbing Code and the International Plumbing Code.
***EPAct 1992 standard for toilets applies to both commercial and residential models.
****Residential shower stall in dwelling units:
  - Where the floor area of the shower compartment is less than 2,500 sq. in, the total allowable flow rate from all flowing showerheads at any given time, including rain systems, waterfalls, bodysprays, bodyspas, and jets shall be limited to the allowable showerhead flow rate as specified above, i.e. 2.5 gpm, per shower stall.
  - For each increment of 2,500 sq. in. of floor area thereafter or part thereof, an additional showerhead shall be allowed, the total allowable flow rate from all flowing devices equal to or less than the allowable flow rate as specified above.
  - Exception: Showers that emit recirculated non-potable water originating from within the shower stall while operating are allowed to exceed the maximum as long as the total potable water flow does not exceed the flow rate as specified above.

The following fixtures, fittings and appliances are outside the scope of the water use reduction calculation:

- Commercial Steam Cookers
- Commercial Dishwashers
- Automatic Commercial Ice Makers
- Commercial (family-sized) Clothes Washers
- Residential Clothes Washers
- Standard and Compact Residential Dishwashers

Although water–efficient dishwashers, laundry machines, etc cannot be included in the calculations for this credit, they may be included in the exemplary performance calculations in WE Credit 3.

UPC and IPC Standards for Plumbing Fixture Water Use

Fixture	UPC and IPC Standards	EPA WaterSense Standards
Water closets (gpf)	1.60	1.28
Urinals (gpf)	1.00	0.50[a]
Showerheads (gpm*)	2.50	1.5 - 2.0[b]
Public lavatory faucets and aerators (gpm**)	0.50	
Private lavatory faucets and aerators (gpm**)	2.20	1.50
Public metering lavatory faucets (gal per cycle)	0.25	
Kitchen and janitor sink faucets (gpm)	2.20	
Metering faucets (gal per cycle)	0.25	

*When measured at 80 psi
**When measured at 60 psi
[a] On 5/22/08, the EPA issued a notification of intent to develop a specification for high-efficiency urinals. WaterSense anticipates establishing a maximum allowable flush volume of 0.5 gpf.
[b] On 8/30/07, the EPA issued a notification of intent to develop a specification for showerheads. WaterSense anticipates establishing a single maximum flow rate between 1.5 gpm and 2.0 gpm.

- Identify the number of occupants by type:
  - **NC, C&S**: Full-time staff, Part-time staff, Transients (students, visitors, retail customers), Residents
  - **Schools**: Full-time staff, Part-time staff, Students, Transients (volunteers, visitors, etc.).
- Use FTE hrs where an 8 hr occupant has a value of 1 for a 40 hr week, part-time has a value of hrs/day/8; in buildings with shifts, use the number of FTEs from all shifts and FTE hrs for shifts should be applied consistently for all credits.
- See Tables 2 and 3 for Default Fixture Uses by Occupant Type.

Technology and Strategy:

- **WaterSense-certified fixtures and fixture fittings should be used where available.**
- **WaterSense is sponsored by the EPA, helps consumers, and exceeds the UPC and the IPC in some cases.**
- Use high efficiency fixtures (water closets, urinals) and dry fixtures e.g. composting toilets to reduce potable water demand.
- Use alternate <u>onsite</u> water sources such as rainwater, stormwater, ac condensate, and graywater for non-potable applications such as toilets/urinals (as approved by manufacturer) and custodial uses.
- Reduce potable water demand through high efficiency or dry fixtures, or occupancy sensors.
- Use stormwater or graywater for non-potable applications.
- Base projects on **Location, Codes and Overall Project Function**.

WaterSense lavatory faucet requirements:	$\leq$ 1.5 gpm at 60 psi, $\geq$ 0.8 gpm at 20 psi
WaterSense urinals:	$\leq$ 0.5 gal/flush
WaterSense tank-type single-flush:	$\leq$ 1.28 gal/flush avg flush volume
WaterSense tank-type dual-flush:	$\leq$ 1.28 gal/flush composite, avg flush vol of 2 reduced flushes & 1 full flushes
WaterSense showerheads:	$\leq$ 1.5 – 2.0 gpm

Timeline/Team: Predesign – Owner, Architect, Engineer; Design Development – Engineering Team; Construction Documents – Owner, Architect; Construction – Design Team, Owner, Contractor.

Regional Variations: Local building and health codes differ in their treatment of alternative plumbing fixtures.
O&M Considerations: Consider submeters for fixtures or fittings, special cleaning and maintenance, and special maintenance.

WE Credit 1 Water Efficient Landscaping (2-4, 2-4, 2-4)

Intent: Limit or eliminate the use of potable water, or other natural surface or subsurface water resources available on or near the project site, for landscape irrigation.

Requirements:

OPTION 1: **Reduce by 50% (2 points)**

Reduce potable water consumption for irrigation by 50% from a calculated mid-summer baseline by any combination of:

- Plant species factor, density factor and microclimate factor
- Irrigation efficiency
- Captured rainwater
- Recycled wastewater
- Water treated and conveyed by a public agency specifically for non-potable uses

Technology and Strategy:

- Perform a soil/climate analysis to determine appropriate plant material and design the landscape with native or adapted plants to reduce or eliminate irrigation requirements
- Where irrigation is required, use high-efficiency equipment and/or climate-based controllers
- Use groundwater seepage that is pumped away from the immediate vicinity of building slabs and foundations if it can be demonstrated that doing so does not affect site stormwater management systems.

OPTION 2: **No Potable Water Use or Irrigation* (4 points)**

*If the **% reduction** of **potable** water is **100% AND** the **% reduction** of **total water** is $\geq$ **50%**, **both Option1 and Option 2 are earned and 4 points are awarded.**

Requirements:

Achieve Option 1 and:

PATH 1

Use **only** captured rainwater, recycled wastewater, recycled graywater, or water treated and conveyed by a public agency specifically for non-potable uses for irrigation.

OR

PATH 2

Install landscaping that does **not require** permanent irrigation systems (temporary systems allowed for only 1 year).

Technology and Strategy:

- Perform a soil/climate analysis to determine appropriate plant material and design the landscape with native or adapted plants to reduce or eliminate irrigation requirements.
- Use stormwater, graywater and/or condensate water for irrigation.
- Create a landscape that maximizes the use of on-site natural resources to limit or eliminate use of potable water for irrigation.

WE Credit 1 (cont.)

Recommended Design Principals: climate-tolerant plants, direct runoff and minimal turf

<u>Most effective strategy to reduce irrigation water cost is landscaping adapted to local climate and site's microclimate</u>

Step 1. Planning and design
- Site map showing structures, topography, orientation, sun & wind exposure, use of space, existing vegetation
- Shadow profiles of landscape areas for each season based on middle of day conditions showing plant selection
- Reduce heat island effect through shading; plant hard wood trees to increase shade canopy

Step 2. Practical turf areas
- Plant turf grasses only for functional benefits, e.g. recreation, pedestrians, conservation

Step 3. Soil analysis and preparation
- Analyze soil in each zone
- Amend soil accordingly

Step 4. Appropriate use of plants, i.e. plants that will easily adapt to the site
- Consider the mature size and form for the location and purpose
- Consider the growth rate
- Determine that texture and color are right for surrounding plantings and building background
- Use no mono-species or excessive multi-species selections
- Diversify species to prevent elimination of a species from diseases or pest infestation

Step 5. Effective and efficient watering practices
- Regularly check irrigation systems' efficiency and effectiveness; verify watering schedules on a monthly basis
- Use drip, micro misters and subsurface systems where applicable
- Use smart irrigation controllers and provide computer interface for monitoring and scheduling from central locale
- No irrigation of plants and turf from November to April

Step 6. Use mulch on trees, shrubs and flower beds
- Keep landscape areas mulched to conserve moisture and prevent evaporation from the soil surface

Technologies: irrigation technology, rainwater capture, advanced wastewater treatment

- Irrigation tech: Micro systems (drips are 90% efficient and sprinklers are 62.5% efficient; drips use 30-50% less), moisture sensors, rain shut-offs, and weather based evapotranspiration controllers
- Rainwater collection: cisterns, underground tanks, ponds (use screens or filters; asphalt or lead-containing is bad)
- Waste-water recovery: on site (water with no human waste or food processing) or at municipal level (tertiary)

Calculations:

<u>Based on the month of **July**</u>

$K_L =$ K_s x K_d x K_{mc} = for each landscape area (trees, shrubs, groundcover, turf and mixed)

$K_L =$ landscape coefficient = volume of water lost via evapotranspiration, dependent on species, microclimate, density

$K_s =$ species factor = variation of water needs according to plant species

$K_d =$ density factor = number of plants and the total leaf area of a landscape

$K_{mc} =$ microclimate factor = environmental conditions specific to the landscape, e.g. temp, wind and humidity

$ET_0 =$ evapotranspiration rate = measure of the total amount of <u>water needed to grow a reference plant</u> (grass/alfalfa)

$ET_L =$ ET_0 x K_L = project specific rate for each landscape area

$IE =$ Irrigation Efficiency for the type of irrigation used, e.g. sprinkler, drip, etc

$CE =$ Controller Efficiency = % reduced water use from weather-based controller or moisture sensor-based system

Reuse Water Volume = captured rain, recycled graywater and/or treated wastewater

TWA = total water applied (gal)

TWPA = total potable water applied (gal)

WE Credit 1 (cont.)

Calculations (cont.)

STEP 1 – Create **Design Case**

- Sort total landscape area (within the site boundary) into Trees, Shrubs, Groundcover, Turf and Mixed (by square feet)
- For each area type, determine Factors from low, average or high values as appropriate for the design
- Calculate K_L
- Determine ET_0 for July for the region (in <u>inches</u>)
- Calculate ET_L
- Determine IE
- Determine CE <u>if applicable</u>
- Calculate Reuse Water volume
- Calculate <u>Design TWA</u> for <u>each landscape area</u> $\textbf{TWA}_{\textbf{design}}$ = **Area x (ET_L/IE)** <u>**x CE**</u> **x 0.6233** <u>**gal/ft2/in**</u>
- Calculate <u>Design TWPA</u> for <u>each landscape area</u> $\textbf{TWPA}_{\textbf{design}}$ = $\textbf{TWA}_{\textbf{design}}$ **- Reuse**

STEP 2 – Create **Baseline Case**

- Set K_s, K_d and IE to <u>average values for conventional equipment and design practices</u>
- Use same K_{mc} and reference ET_0 values in Design and Baseline cases
- Account for substitution of low-water using landscape types of plants by reallocating the landscape types
- Calculate <u>Baseline TWA</u> for <u>each landscape area</u> $\textbf{TWA}_{\textbf{baseline}}$ = **Area x (ET_L/IE) x 0.6233** <u>**gal/ft2/in**</u>
- Note: **Reuse is zero for the baseline.** Therefore, $\textbf{TWPA}_{\textbf{baseline}}$ = $\textbf{TWA}_{\textbf{baseline}}$

STEP 3 – Calculate **% Reduction in Potable** Water Use **for Irrigation, and** the **% Reduction in Total Irrigation** Water (Potable and Reuse)

- Calculate % reduction in potable water use   = (1 – Design TWPA/Baseline TWA) x 100; **need 50% for Option 1**
- **If 100%**, calculate % reduction of total water use = (1 – Design TWA/Baseline TWA) x 100; **need 50% for Option 2**

Exemplary Performance: na

Design Submittal:

- LEED Online
- Calculate baseline and design water demand
- Report what portion of irrigation will come from each nonpotable source, if any.
- Prepare a landscape plan showing a planting schedule and irrigation system.

Timeline/Team: Design – Landscape Designer, Owner, Architect, Civil Engineer, Mechanical Engineer, Maintenance Staff

Regional Variations:
- Consider the site's climate, microclimate, sun exposure, soil type, drainage and topography
- Hot & Dry Climates: drought-tolerant plants, xeriscape, little or no turfgrasses, rocks and stones
- Hot & Humid: native plants, rain or moisture sensors, captured rain
- Cold Climates: hardy native plants, rain or moisture sensors

O&M Considerations:
- Submetering
- Site landscape maintenance plan
- Graywater systems may require special maintenance
- Guidance for temporary irrigation for plant establishment

WE Credit 2 Innovative Wastewater Technologies (2, 2, 2)

Intent: Reduce generation of wastewater and potable water demand, while increasing the local aquifer recharge.

Requirements:

OPTION 1

Reduce potable water use for building sewage conveyance by **50%** through the use of:

- water-conserving fixtures (water closets, urinals)
- non-potable water (captured rainwater, recycled graywater, on-site or municipally treated wastewater)

OPTION 2

Treat 50% of wastewater on-site to tertiary standards; **must be infiltrated or used on-site**

Tertiary Treatment:	highest form; removal of nutrients, organic and solid material, plus biological or chemical polishing
Non-water Urinal:	no flush; trap with layer of buoyant liquid that floats above urine layer blocking sewer gas and odor
Non-potable Water:	not suitable human consumption without treatment that meets or exceeds EPA drinking standards
Potable Water:	meets or exceeds EPA's drinking water quality standards and is approved for human consumption
Process Water:	used for industrial processes and building systems, e.g. cooling towers, boilers, and chillers; used for operational process, e.g. dishwashing, clothes washing, and ice making (See WE Cr3 Ex. Performance)

Technology and Strategy:

OPTION 1:
- High efficiency fixtures and dry fixtures (composting toilets and waterless urinals) to reduce waste water
- Reuse stormwater or graywater for sewage conveyance

OPTION 2:
- Packaged biological nutrient removal systems
- Constructed wetlands
- High-efficiency filtration systems

Calculations:

- Calculate FTEs for all shifts and for transients
- **Assume 50% male and 50% female**
- **Males: toilets 1/day, urinals 2/day, sink 3/day**
- **Females: toilets 3/day, sink 3/day**
- Water and rainwater reuse volumes must be <u>sufficient to meet toilet demands</u> and are subtracted from daily totals
- <u>Baseline</u> case is based on fixture flow rates according the <u>Energy Policy Act of 1992</u> and <u>no water or rainwater harvest</u>
- <u>Rainwater or graywater reuse are</u> given as a <u>negative</u> value <u>in the design case</u>

Exemplary Performance: 100% for either Option 1 <u>or</u> Option 2

Design Submittal

Timeline/Team: Predesign – Owner, Architect, Engineer; Schematic Design – Mechanical Engineers; Design Development – Engineering Team; Construction Documents – Owner, Architect; Construction – Design Team, Owner, Contractor.

Regional Variations: Consider local climate and weather when considering rainwater harvesting and on-site wastewater treatment; Consider local regulations and permits.

O&M Considerations: Educate owners and managers; train the maintenance staff

WE Credit 3 Water Use Reduce Reduction (2-4, 2-4, 2-4)

Intent: See WE Prerequisite 1
Requirements: See WE Prerequisite 1

A total of 2 to 4 points can be earned by reducing building water use. Points are awarded as follows:
* **30% reduction: 2 points**
* **35% reduction: 3 points**
* **40% reduction: 4 points**

National Efficiency Baselines for Commercial Water-Using Fixtures, Fittings and Appliances

Fixtures, Fittings and Appliances	Current Baseline
Commercial Toilets	1.6 gpf* except blow-out fixtures: 3.5 gpf
Commercial Urinals	1.0 gpf
Commercial Lavatory (restroom) Faucets	2.2 gpm at 60 psi – private applications only (hotel/motel guest rooms, hospital patient rooms) 0.5 gpm at 60 psi** – all others except private applications 0.25 gallons per cycle for metering faucets
Commercial Pre-rinse Spray Valves (for food service applications)	Flow rate ≤ 1.6 gpm (no pressure specified; no performance requirement)

National Efficiency Baselines for Residential Water-Using Fixtures, Fittings and Appliances

Fixtures, Fittings and Appliances	Current Baseline
Residential Toilets	1.6 gpf***
Residential Lavatory (Bathroom) Faucets	2.2 gpm at 60 psi
Residential Kitchen Faucet	
Residential Showerheads	2.5 gpm at 80 psi per shower stall****

*EPAct 1992 standard for toilets applies to both commercial and residential models
**In addition to EPAct requirements, ASME standard for public lavatory faucets is 0.5 gpm at 60 psi. This maximum has been incorporated into the national Uniform Plumbing Code and the International Plumbing Code.
***EPAct 1992 standard for toilets applies to both commercial and residential models.
****Residential shower stall in dwelling units:
   o   Where the floor area of the shower compartment is less than 2,500 sq. in, the total allowable flow rate from all flowing showerheads at any given time, including rain systems, waterfalls, bodysprays, bodyspas, and jets shall be limited to the allowable showerhead flow rate as specified above, i.e. 2.5 gpm, per shower stall.
   o   For each increment of 2,500 sq. in. of floor area thereafter or part thereof, an additional showerhead shall be allowed, the total allowable flow rate from all flowing devices equal to or less than the allowable flow rate as specified above.
   o   Exception: Showers that emit recirculated non-potable water originating from within the shower stall while operating are allowed to exceed the maximum as long as the total potable water flow does not exceed the flow rate as specified above.

The following fixtures, fittings and appliances are outside the scope of the water use reduction calculation but may be used in the Exemplary Performance calculations for this credit (along with non-regulated eqpt, e.g. cooling towers, etc):
* Commercial Steam Cookers
* Commercial Dishwashers
* Automatic Commercial Ice Makers
* Commercial (family-sized) Clothes Washers
* Residential Clothes Washers
* Standard and Compact Residential Dishwashers

Technology and Strategy: See WE Prerequisite 1
Exemplary Performance: 45% reduction in projected potable water use (may use dishwashers, cooling towers, etc).
Design Submittal
Timeline/Team: See WE Prerequisite 1
Regional Variations: See WE Prerequisite 1
O&M Considerations: See WE Prerequisite 1

WE Credit 4 Process Water Use Reduction (0, 1, 0)

Intent (for Schools only): To maximize water efficiency within buildings to reduce the burden on municipal water supply and wastewater systems.

Requirements:

- **No** refrigeration equipment using **once-through cooling** with potable water
- **No garbage disposals**
- **At least 4 process items** where water use is at or below the levels shown in the table below.
- Inclusion of equipment not listed must show a documented 20% reduction in water use from a benchmark or industry standard

Equipment Type	Maximum Water Use	Other Requirements
Clothes washers*	7.5 gal/ft^3/cycle	
Dishwashers with racks	1.0 gal/rack	
Ice machines**	lbs/day>175 20 gal/100lbs	No water-cooled machines
	lbs/day>175 30 gal/100lbs	No water-cooled machines
Food steamers	2 gal/hr	Boilerless steamers only
Prerinse spray valves	1.4 gpm	

*Commercial CEE Tier 3a – Residential CEE Tier 1
**CEE Tier 3

Technology and Strategy:

- Save water, energy and chemicals by reducing potable water use.
- Garbage disposals introduce unprocessed food waste into the municipal water system and increase biochemical O_2 demand.
- Reducing water and energy demand can reduce construction costs, taxes, and rates.
- Assess all processes in the building that use water.
- Address the equipment listed above.
- Other equipment not included in other WE credits, i.e. non-regulated equipment, must achieve a 20% reduction in water use over an acceptable benchmark or industry standard.
- If the equipment does not have an established baseline, other industry standards or benchmarks must be cited; the proposed baselines will be evaluated on a case-by-case basis.

Calculations:

- No calculations are required if the equipment has a baseline established in the credit requirements.
- Equipment not listed must establish a new baseline and demonstrate the equipment reduces process water by at least 20%.
- Example: A closed-loop cooling tower can reduce the need for potable water; the contaminant-free closed loop reduces the potable water use compared with a traditional once-through cooling system.

Exemplary Performance: achieve a projected process water savings of 40%.

Design Submittal:

- Retain documents showing the manufacturer, model, and water consumption rates of each appliance.
- Assemble info about the baseline water use based on industry standards or benchmarks for equipment not listed in this credit.

Timeline/Team: Design Development and Construction Documents – Owner, Architect

Regional Variations: na

O&M Considerations: Ensure that operators receive design documents (for refrigeration equipment) and manufacturers' specifications on installed equipment. Submeter process water consumption if possible.

Energy and Atmosphere NC 11-35 Pts, Schools 9-33 Pts, C&S 19-37 Pts

- Buildings consume 39% of the energy and 74% of the electricity produced in the US.
- Generating electricity from fossil fuels (oil, gas, coal) affects the environment at each step of production and use.

- Coal mining disrupts habitats and can devastate landscapes.
- Coal-fired plants accounted for over 50% of the US electricity generation in 2006.
- Each MW of coal-generated electricity releases 2,249 lbs of CO_2, 13 lbs of SO_2 and 6 lbs of NO_x.
- Over 65% of SO_2 released in the air is from electricity generation.

- Natural gas, nuclear fission and hydroelectric generators have adverse environmental consequences as well.
- Gas is a major source of NO and greenhouse gas emissions.
- Nuclear power increases the potential for catastrophic accidents and has waste transportation and disposal issues.
- Hydroelectric generating plants disrupt natural waterflows and disturb aquatic habitats.

- Green buildings reduce the amount of energy required and use more benign forms of energy.
- Better energy performance reduces greenhouse gas emission and results in lower operating costs.
- Electricity generation using sources other than fossil fuels reduces the environmental impacts of building energy use.

Energy Performance
- The most effective way to optimize energy efficiency is to use an integrated, whole building approach.
- Massing, orientation, materials, construction methods, envelope, water efficiency, HVAC and lighting determine efficiency.
- Green schools provide a unique opportunity for students to explore the interdependence of system, design and performance.

The Energy and Atmosphere section of the GBD&C Reference Guide promotes three kinds of activities:

Tracking Building Energy Performance – Designing, Commissioning, Monitoring
- Projects must at a minimum perform better than the average building.
- The building must be designed for high performance, commissioned to ensure construction meets design intent, and monitored (measurement and verification) to ensure long-term performance.
- **Design** must be based on designated mandatory and prescriptive requirements of 90.1-2007 or USGBC-approved local codes, whichever is more stringent.
- Optimization beyond 90.1-2007 is required in EA Pr2 through simulation modeling or prescriptive options.
- **Commissioning (Cx)**: develop the OPRs, create a formal Cx plan, verify equipment installation, and submit a final report.
- Enhanced Cx: review design and contractor submittals, create a formal systems manual, verify staff training, perform a follow-up review before the warranty period ends.
- Cx can help ensure that indoor environmental quality is properly maintained.
- **Monitoring** begins with establishing an M&V plan based on IPMVP best practices.
- The plan must cover at least one year of post-construction occupancy, involve appropriate measuring instrumentation, and can include the energy use simulation.

Managing Refrigerants to Eliminate CFCs
- **Release of CFCs** from refrigeration equipment **destroys ozone molecules in the <u>stratosphere</u>** through a catalytic process.
- Ozone depletion harms the Earth's natural shield from incoming UV radiation.
- **CFCs** in the stratosphere **also absorb infrared radiation and create chlorine**, a potent greenhouse gas.
- Do not install equipment with CFCs; use refrigerants with low ODP and GWP.

Using Renewable Energy
- Use **on-site renewable energy** systems and buy **off-site green power**.
- On-site: **electrical** (PV, wind, hydro, wave, tidal, biofuel), **geothermal** (water, steam), **solar thermal** (collection, storage).
- Off-site: contract for a minimum **purchase of green power**.
- Renewable alternatives may be less expensive than traditional power in some areas.
- Some states allow <u>net metering</u> which can offset onsite renewable energy costs by <u>selling excess electricity back to the utility</u>.

EA Prerequisite 1 Fundamental Commissioning of Building Energy Systems

Intent: Verify that the project's energy related systems are installed, calibrated and performing according to the owner's project requirements, basis of design and construction documents.

<u>Benefits of Commissioning</u>: Reduced energy use, lower operating costs, reduced contractor callbacks, better building documentation, improved occupant productivity, and verification that the systems perform in accordance with the owner's project requirements

Requirements: The following Commissioning Process activities shall be <u>completed by the</u> Project <u>Team</u>:

1. Designate a <u>Commissioning Authority (CxA)</u> to lead, review and oversee completion of the commissioning process activities:

    a) CxA must have documented CxA experience in at least 2 building projects.

    b) CxA must be independent of the project's design and construction management, but may be an employee of the any firms providing those services; CxA may be a qualified employee or consultant of the Owner.

    c) CxA must report results, findings and recommendations directly to the Owner.

    d) For projects smaller than 50,000 ft^2 gross, the CxA may be a qualified person on the design or construction teams who has the required experience.

2. Owner must document the Owner's Project Requirements (OPR). Design Team shall develop the Basis of Design (BOD). The CxA shall review these documents. Owner and Design Team shall update their respective documents.

3. Develop and incorporate commissioning requirements into the construction documents.

4. Develop and implement a commissioning plan.

5. Verify the installation and performance of the systems to be commissioned.

6. Complete a summary commissioning report.

Commissioning must be performed for the following energy-related systems, at a minimum:

- HVAC&R (mechanical and passive) and associated controls
- Lighting and daylighting controls
- Domestic hot water systems
- Renewable energy systems (wind, solar, etc.)

Technology and Strategy:

- Engage a CxA prior to start of design
- Determine the Owner's program and initial design intent
- Develop and maintain a commissioning plan for use during design and construction
- Incorporate commissioning requirements in bid documents
- Assemble the commissioning team and, prior to occupancy, verify performance of the energy consuming systems
- Complete the commissioning reports with recommendations prior to acceptance of the HVAC systems

Timeline/Team:

- The Cx process is most effective when begun at project inception.
- It is a planned, systematic, quality-control process involving the owner, users, occupants, O&M staff, designers, contractors.
- A team approach can speed up the process and add a system of checks and balances.
- The overall Cx effort is divided into 12 steps (see Table 1, p. 220). Some steps are required for EA Pr1, some for EA Cr3.

EA Prerequisite 1 (cont.)

The following Cx process steps are presented sequentially, however some steps can be begin or end at various project stages.

Step 1. Designate CxA
- The CxA is responsible for directing the Cx team and Cx process in the completion of the Cx requirements.
- The CxA is responsible for coordinating, overseeing, and/or performing the Cx testing.
- The CxA is responsible for reviewing the results of the systems performance verification

Step 2. Document Owner's Project Requirements (OPRs) and Develop Basis of Design (BOD):

Owner's Project Requirements:
- Owner and User Requirements
- Environmental and Sustainability Goals
- Energy Efficiency Goals
- Indoor Environmental Quality Requirements
- Equipment and System Expectations
- Building Occupant and O&M Personnel Requirements

Basis of Design (BOD):
- Primary Design Assumptions
- Standards
- Narrative Descriptions

Step 3. Review OPRs and BOD:
- The CxA must review the OPRs and BOD for clarity and completeness.
- The owner and design team are responsible for updates to their respective documents.
- The CxA must ensure that the BOD reflects the OPRs.
- Both documents must be reviewed by the CxA for completeness prior to the approval of contractor submittals for any commissioned equipment or systems.

Step 4. Develop and Implement Commissioning Plan:
- Commissioning Program Overview
- Commissioning Team
- Commissioning Process Activities
- Document the commissioning review process **(if pursuing EA Cr3)**
- Review contractor submittals **(if pursuing EA Cr3)**
- Develop the systems manual **(if pursuing EA Cr3)**
- Verify the training of operations personnel **(if pursuing EA Cr3)**
- Review building operation after final acceptance

Step 5. Incorporate Commissioning Requirements into Construction Documents:
- The project specifications are used to inform contractors of their responsibilities in the Cx process.
- Cx requirements may be outlined in a section of the general conditions of the construction specifications.
- Placing all Cx requirements in a single location gives Cx work responsibility to the GC, who can assign work to subs.
- It is valuable to refer to Cx requirements in the drawings, bid forms and spec sections related to commissioned systems.

Step 6. Conduct Commissioning Design Review Prior to Mid-Construction Documents:
- The CxA should conduct at least 1 Cx design review of the OPRs, BOD and design documents prior to the mid-construction documents phase and back-check the review comments in the subsequent design submission.
- **This step is not mandatory for EA Pr1, but it is required for EA Cr3.**
- The CxA should provide an independent assessment of the state of the design for the commissioned systems as follows:

Step 7. Review Contractor Submittals Applicable to Systems Being Commissioned:
- The CxA should review contractor submittals applicable to commissioned systems for compliance with OPRs & BOD.
- **This step is not mandatory for EA Pr1, but it is required for EA Cr3.**
- The CxA should identify issues that might otherwise result in rework or change orders.

EA Prerequisite 1 (cont.)

Step 8. Verify Installation and Performance of Commissioned Systems:
- Installation Inspections
- System Performance Testing
- Evaluation of results compared to the OPR and BOD

Step 9. Develop Systems Manual for Commissioned Systems:
- Final version of the BOD
- System single-line diagrams
- As-build sequences of operations, control drawings and original setpoints
- Operating instructions for integrated building systems
- Recommended schedule of maintenance requirements and frequency, if not already in the project O&M manuals
- Recommended schedule of retesting of commissioned systems with blank test forms from the original Cx plan
- Recommended schedule for calibrating sensors and actuators

Step10. Verify that Requirements for Training Are Completed:
- Establish and document training expectations and needs with the owner.
- **This step is not mandatory for EA Pr1, but it is required for EA Cr3**.
- Document that the training was completed according to the contract documents.
- Have a contract in place to review operation with O&M staff and occupants.
- Have a **plan in the contract for resolution of outstanding Cx related issues within 10 months after substantial completion**.

Step11. Complete a Summary Commissioning Report:
- After installation inspections and performance verification
- Executive summary of the process and the results of the commissioning program
- A history of any system deficiencies identified and how they were resolved
- Systems performance test results and evaluation
- Summary of the design review process **(if pursuing EA Cr3)**
- Summary of the submittal review process **(if pursuing EA Cr3)**
- Summary of the O&M documentation and training process **(if pursuing EA Cr3)**

Step12. Review Building Operation Within 10 Months After Substantial Completion:
- Review building operation 10 months after substantial completion with O&M staff and occupants.
- Have a plan for resolving outstanding issues.
- **This step is not mandatory for EA Pr1, but it is required for EA Cr3**.
- All unresolved construction deficiencies should be documented and corrected under manufac. or contractor warranties.
- ID any problems with operating the building as originally intended and ID uncorrectable issues in the systems manual.

Though the commissioning process should start as early in the design process as possible, it is allowable to engage a Cx agent to execute fundamental commissioning after construction has begun.

Calculations: na

Exemplary Performance: na

Construction Submittal

Regional Variations: The significance of commissioning may vary with climate, e.g. commissioning water systems in arid climates or commissioning of building envelopes in certain regions.

O&M Considerations: Use the Cx process to develop documents to help facility managers run the building consistent with the design intent and equipment specs: building operation plan (OPRs), systems narrative, sequence of operations, preventative maintenance plan, Cx report.

EA Prerequisite 2 Minimum Energy Performance

Intent: Establish the minimum level of energy efficiency for the proposed building and systems to reduce environmental and economic impacts associated with excessive energy use.

Requirements:

OPTION 1 – WHOLE BUILDING ENERGY SIMULATION

- **10%** improvement over 90.1-2007 (with errata, without addenda) for new buildings, **5% for existing** building renovations.
- **Whole building simulation** using the Building Performance Rating Method in Appendix G of 90.1-2007.
- Baseline must comply with **Appendix G**.
- Design must comply with **mandatory** Sections (5.4, 6.4, 7.4, 8.4, 9.4, 10.4) of <u>90.1-2007</u> (w errata, w/o addenda).
- Energy analysis must include ALL energy costs <u>within and associated with</u> the building project.

- **Default process energy cost is 25%** of the total energy cost for the baseline building.
- If actual process energy cost is less than 25% of the baseline total, submit supporting documentation to substantiate.
- Process loads are identical for both the baseline and proposed building unless there are measures to reduce them.
- **Exceptional Calculation Method** (90.1-2007 G2.5) can be used to <u>document measures to reduce process loads</u>.
- Documentation of process load energy savings shall include baseline and design assumptions, and supporting theory and calculations.

OPTION 2 – PRESCRIPTIVE COMPLIANCE PATH: <u>Advanced Energy Design Guide</u>

<u>New Construction and Core Shell</u>:

Comply with all the **prescriptive measures** and **climate zone criteria** in the applicable Advanced Energy Design Guide:

Path 1. ASHRAE Advanced Energy Design Guide for **Small Office** Buildings 2004:
   Buildings must be **< 20,000 ft^2**
   Buildings must be **office occupancy**
Path 2. ASHRAE Advanced Energy Design Guide for **Small Retail** Buildings 2006: must be **< 20,000 ft^2**
Path 3. ASHRAE Advanced Energy Design Guide for **Small Warehouses & Self Storage** Buildings 2008: must be **< 50,000 ft^2**

<u>Schools</u>:

- Comply with all the **prescriptive measures** and **climate zone criteria** in the ASHRAE Advanced Energy Design Guide for **K-12 School Buildings.**

OPTION 3 – PRESCRIPTIVE COMPLIANCE PATH: <u>Advanced Buildings Core Performance Guide</u>

- Comply with prescriptive measures in the Advanced Buildings Core Performance Guide by the New Buildings Institute:
- Buildings must be **< 100,000 ft^2**
- Buildings may **not** be **healthcare, warehouse or laboratory projects.**
- Comply with Section One: Design Process Strategies, <u>and</u> Section Two: Core Performance Requirements.
- Office, school, public assembly and retail projects must comply with Sections One and Two.
- All other projects (no health care, warehouse, laboratory projects) must implement the basic requirements of the Guide.

EA Prerequisite 2 (cont.)

Technology and Strategy:

- Design building envelope and systems to meet baseline requirements.
- Computer simulation to assess energy performance and identify the most cost-effective energy efficiency measures.
- Quantify energy performance as compared to a baseline building.
- If a local code has demonstrated quantitative and textual equivalence following, at a minimum, the US Dept of Energy process for commercial energy code determination, the results of that analysis may be used to correlate local code performance with 90.1-2007.
- Approved ASHRAE addenda may be used for this prerequisite, but must be applied consistently <u>across all credits</u>.

Calculations: Follow calculation and documentation methodology in 90.1-2007 (w errata, w/o addenda)

- A conditioned **conservatory or greenhouse space** cannot be excluded on the basis of horticulture "process loads" when it qualifies as an amenity for the occupants or users of the facility rather than as the primary facility function; conditioning for the space must be included in the energy simulation and savings calculations.
- **Gross floor area** of a building includes both conditioned and unconditioned spaces; if the area exceeds 25,000 ft^2, HVAC systems must comply with mandatory requirements of Section 6.4; only those areas heated or cooled per Section 2.2(1) must meet the envelope requirements.
- **Lighting power calculations** must use either the building area method or the space-by-space method; for either method, actual total installed interior lighting power is the sum of all <u>permanently installed</u> general, task and furniture lighting (lamps, ballasts, regulators and controls wattages).
- To establish the **baseline for the lighting power calculations**:
    - Use the **building area method** if the project is for the entire building or single independent occupancy within a multi-occupancy building: interior area x allowable lighting power density (Table 9.5.1), or
    - For the **space-by-space method**: interior area x allowable LPD (Table 9.5.1 by "space type")
    - For each **exterior surface**: area or length of each surface x allowable LPD (Table 9.4.5) x 1.05

Exemplary Performance: na

Design Submittal

Timeline/Team: Project team should start energy modeling early in the Design Phase.

Regional Variations: Regional variance is presented in 90.1-2007 for 8 climate zones and 3 subzones; this accounts for minimum envelope and glazing requirements for each climate type.

O&M Considerations: Ensure systems are functioning properly and track energy use. Promote energy efficiency; provide management with a baseline of energy end uses from the model; utilize Energy Star software tools.

EA Prerequisite 3 Fundamental Refrigerant Management

Intent: Reduce stratospheric ozone depletion.

Requirements:

- Zero use of CFC-based refrigerants in new base building HVAC&R systems

- When reusing existing base building HVAC equipment, complete a comprehensive CFC phase-out conversion prior to project completion. Phase-out plans extending beyond the project completion date will be considered on the merits.

Technology and Strategy:

- Choose refrigerants with short environmental lifetimes, small ODP values and small GWP values.

- When reusing existing HVAC: inventory equipment and provide replacement schedule for CFC refrigerants.

- For new buildings: specify new HVAC equipment in the base building that uses no CFC refrigerants.

- Replace or retrofit any CFC-using equipment in the base building HVAC&R and Fire Suppressant Systems.

- If bldg(s) are connected to an existing CHW system:

  1. The existing system must be **CFC free**, OR

  2. Have **5-yr phase-out plan**, and reduce **CFC leakage to $\leq$ 5%/yr** using the **EPA Clean Air Act as a guide**, OR

  3. A **third party** must conduct an **audit to show replacement or conversion** of existing equipment **is not economically feasible** (i.e. payback > 10 yrs), and reduce **CFC leakage to $\leq$ 5%/yr** using the **EPA Clean Air Act as a guide**.

- Minimize refrigerant leakage. Under Section 608 of the EPA's Clean Air Act of 1990:
  - Require practices that maximize recycling of ODP compounds during service and disposal of equipment.
  - Set certification requirements for recycle/recovery equipment, techs and reclaimers; prohibit sale to uncertified techs
  - Require persons servicing/disposing AC or refrigeration equipment to certify with the EPA that they have acquired recycle/recovery equipment and are complying with rule.
  - Require repair of substantial leaks in equipment with refrigerant charge > 50 lbs.
  - Establish safe disposal requirements, e.g. remove refrigerants from waste goods having intact charges (car AC, window units, refrigerators, etc.).
  - Prohibit knowingly discharging ODP compounds (CFCs, HFCs) during maintenance or disposal.

Calculations: na

Exemplary Performance: na

Design Submittal

Timeline/Team: Mechanical Engineer, Specialist and Owner develop phase-out plan.

Regional Variations: na

O&M Considerations: Provide facility operators with complete records (e.g. a LEED application) of phase out plans; ensure equipment labels are in place and accessible.

EA Credit 1 Optimize Energy Performance (1-19, 1-19, 3-21)

Intent: Achieve increasing levels of energy performance above the baseline in the prerequisite standard to reduce environmental and economic impacts associated with excessive energy use.

Requirements: (Note: documented achievement of Options 1, 2 or 3 indicates compliance with EA Prerequisite 2)

OPTION 1 – WHOLE BUILDING ENERGY SIMULATION **(1-19, 1-19, 3-21)**

Demonstrate a percentage improvement in the proposed building energy performance rating versus baseline building performance by a whole building project **simulation** using Appendix G of the standard **90.1-2007** (with errata, without addenda).

Points are awarded for New and Existing Building percentage improvement as follows:

New Bldg %	12	14	16	18	20	22	24	26	28	30	32	34	36	38	40	42	44	46	48
Existing Bldg %	8	10	12	14	16	18	20	22	24	26	28	30	32	34	36	38	40	42	44
Points NC, Schools	1	2	3	4	5	6	7	8	9	10	11	12	13	14	15	16	17	18	19
Points C&S	3	4	5	6	7	8	9	10	11	12	13	14	15	16	17	18	19	20	21

- The design must comply with **mandatory** Sections (5.4, 6.4, 7.4, 8.4, 9.4, 10.4) of 90.1-2007 w errata, without addenda.
- The energy analysis must include ALL energy costs within and associated with the building project.
- The design must be compared to a baseline building that complies with **Appendix G** of 90.1-2007 w errata, without addenda.
- **Default process energy cost is 25%** of the total energy cost for the baseline building.
- If the actual process energy cost is less than 25% of the baseline total, submit supporting documentation to substantiate.
- The Performance Rating Method can identify the interactive effects of energy conservation measures.

Process Energy: office/general misc eqpt, computers, elavators/escalators, kitchen eqpt, laundry eqpt, special lighting
Regulated (non-process Energy): lighting, HVAC, and service water heating for domestic or space heating purposes

OPTION 2 – PRESCRIPTIVE COMPLIANCE PATH: <u>**Advanced Energy Design Guide**</u>

<u>**New Construction and Core Shell:**</u>

Comply with all the **prescriptive measures** and **climate zone criteria** in the applicable Advanced Energy Design Guide:

Path 1. ASHRAE Advanced Energy Design Guide for **Small Office** Buildings 2004:
    Buildings must be **< 20,000 ft^2**
    Buildings must be **office occupancy**
Path 2. ASHRAE Advanced Energy Design Guide for **Small Retail** Buildings 2006: must be **< 20,000 ft^2**
Path 3. ASHRAE Advanced Energy Design Guide for **Small Warehouses & Self Storage** Bldgs 2008: must be **< 50,000 ft^2**

<u>**Schools:**</u>

- Comply with all the **prescriptive measures** and **climate zone criteria** in the ASHRAE Advanced Energy Design Guide for **K-12 School Buildings**.

OPTION 3 – PRESCRIPTIVE COMPLIANCE PATH: Advanced Buildings Core **Performance Guide (1-3 Points)**

Comply with prescriptive measures in the Advanced Buildings Core Performance Guide by the New Buildings Institute.

- Buildings must be under **100,000 ft^2**.
- Buildings may **not** be **healthcare, warehouse or laboratory projects**.
- Comply with **Section One**: Design Process Strategies, **and Section Two**: Core Performance Requirements.

- **1 Point** is available for all office, school, public assembly and retail projects <u>comply with Sections One and Two</u>.
- **2 Points** available under **Section 3 Enhanced Performance** at the rate of **1 Point per 3 Strategies** implemented; no <u>points for</u> the following projects: <u>3.1-Cool roofs, 3.8-Night Venting, 3.13-Additional Commissioning (see other Credits)</u>.

EA Credit 1 (cont.)

Technology and Strategy:

- Design building envelope and systems to meet baseline requirements.
- Perform computer simulation to assess energy performance and identify the most cost-effective energy efficiency measures.
- Quantify energy performance as compared to a baseline building.
- If a local code has demonstrated quantitative and textual equivalence following, at a minimum, the US Dept of Energy process for commercial energy code determination, the results of that analysis may be used to correlate local code performance with 90.1-2007.

- Strategies: demand reduction, harvest site energy, increase efficiency, recover waste heat energy
- On-site Renewable Energy: PV, windmills, solar heating panels
- Site Recovery Energy: chiller or DX heat recovery, heat recovery on distribution generator
- Exceptional Calculation Method: use this for measures that cannot be modeled, e.g. on-site renewable energy
- Energy Star Building: comparison to a similar building's performance (score of 50 is the average)

- Approved ASHRAE addenda may be used for this credit, but must be applied consistently across all credits.

Combined Heat and Power (CHP): systems that capture heat that otherwise is wasted in traditional fossil fuel generation of electricity; more efficient, fewer emissions, reduced demand, release of grid capacity, reduced transmission & distribution losses; **4 Cases** are based on (1) Ownership of CHP and Building (2) CHP location (3) Electricity purpose (4) Recovered heat purpose.

Calculations:

- **Opt 1 requires** extensive calculations using **an approved energy simulation program**
    - Input building schedules, orientation, wall/roof/floor data, fenestration data.
    - Input HVAC system type, base system fan power, base system sizing.
    - Run **5 models**: **Base** building **at four 90 degree rotations** and **one Design building**.
    - Use the **average** of **the 4 Base building orientations** for savings calculations.
    - Use **default fenestration at 40% of wall area**, or use actual if less, **uniform for each base orientation**.
    - Use fixed total SA CFM, CV or VAV, for base orientation; reduce static pressure in design to achieve savings.
    - The base building HVAC system is sized using default values.
    - **HVAC** equipment **for base building must be oversized by 15% for cooling and 25% for heating**.
    - The base building lighting should be modeled by "building area" or "space by space", per 90.1-2007.
    - Use **default process energy at 25% unless documented otherwise**.
    - Process loads must be identified for both baseline and proposed performance rating, however, teams may -
    - Use the **Exceptional Calculation Method for measures that can't be modeled**, e.g. process energy savings.
    - Use the **same** utility **rates for base and design** buildings; **"virtual" (blended) rates are acceptable**.
- **Opt 2** uses a prescriptive approach, **does not require a software energy simulation**
    - Use the ASHRAE Advanced Energy Design Guides.
    - Limit building energy use; document improved energy performance.
    - Identify building climate zone location (1 of 8); comply with all recommendations for the climate zone.
- **Opt 3** uses a prescriptive approach, **does not require a software energy simulation**
    - Use Advanced Buildings Core Performance Guide by the New Buildings Institute.
    - Comply with Sections One and Two of the Guide for 1 point and Section Three for up to 2 additional points.

Exemplary Performance: Opt 1 only – New Buildings: 50% improvement; Existing Buildings: 46% improvement.

Design Submittal

Timeline/Team: Schematic Design Phase – simplified model for Architect and Engineer ("shoe box" analysis); Construction Documents Phase – detailed energy model that can be submitted for review – Analyst, Architect, Mechanical Engineer, LEED Consultant, CxA

Regional Variations: already incorporated in 90.1-2007 via 8 climate zones, 3 subzones, and their minimum glazing & envelope requirements

O&M Considerations: Proper building system function and energy use tracking can save energy and operating costs.

EA Credit 2 On-site Renewable Energy (1-7, 1-7, 4)

Intent: Encourage and recognize increasing levels of on-site renewable energy self-supply in order to reduce environmental and economic impacts associated with fossil fuel energy use.

Requirements:

- Use on-site renewable energy systems to offset building energy costs.
- Calculate project performance by expressing renewable system energy production as <u>% of annual energy cost.</u>
- Use the building annual energy cost calculated for EA Credit 1 or use the Deptartment of Energy Commercial Buildings Energy Consumption Survey (CBECS) database to determine the estimated electricity use. If the CBECS is used, also use the Energy Information Administration (EIA) to determine energy costs by state.
- "Virtual" (blended) energy cost rates may be used in absence of actual local utility rates.
- Points awarded are allocated as follows:

New Construction and Schools:

Points	1	2	3	4	5	6	7
Savings	1%	3%	5%	7%	9%	11%	13%

Core & Shell:

Points	4
Savings	1%

- Eligible on-site systems: PV, wind, solar thermal, biofuel, geothermal (heating & electric), hydro (low impact), wave & tidal.
- Ineligible on-site sources: architectural, geo-exchange, passive solar, daylighting or Green Power products from off-site
- <u>Use **net billing** to sell excess power back to the grid.</u>
- <u>Eligible biofuels:</u> untreated wood, waste/mill residue, agricultural crops or waste, animal waste or landfill gas
- <u>Ineligible biofuels:</u> treated wood > 1% of total wood, coated wood, forestry biomass (except mill res.), or municipal solid waste
- <u>Biomass is plant material</u> such as trees, grasses and crops that can be <u>converted to heat energy to produce electricity</u>
- For on-site and off-site sources, the associated environmental attributes must be retained or retired; they cannot be sold.
- For on-site sources, energy exceeding building demand can be sold at the market non-renewable energy rate only.
- If this credit is claimed, Renewable Energy Certificates (RECs) can be sold for the on-site renewable energy system provided (1) RECs equal to 20% of the system's annual rated energy output are purchased from another source, and (2) Seller of the on-site RECs must follow established guidelines and not claim the environmental attributes.

Technology and Strategy:

- Assess the project for non-polluting and renewable energy potential including solar, wind, geothermal, low-impact hydro, biomass and bio-gas strategies
- When applying these strategies, take advantage of **net metering** with local utility companies.

Calculations: use EA Credit 1 simulation calculations or CBECS database as a basis for savings calculations

Exemplary Performance:

- **New Construction and Schools**: 15% or more of annual building energy cost from on-site renewable energy
- **Core & Shell:** 5% or more of annual building energy cost from on-site renewable energy

Design Submittal

Timeline/Team: Project Team, Owner, Architect, and Engineer should first estimate building energy use so renewables with adequate capacity can be identified; design to facilitate net-metering back to grid; ask about incentives and rebates.

Regional Variations: Solar radiation is more abundant in the southwest, biomass more cost-effective in agriculture regions, wind power on the coast.

O&M Considerations: Confirm proper renewable energy system design and implementation, training and O&M guidelines; track renewable production through sub-metering.

EA Credit 3 Enhanced Commissioning (2, 2, 2)

Intent: Begin the commissioning process early during the design process and execute additional activities after systems performance verification is completed.

Requirements:

Implement, or have a contract in place to implement, the following Cx process activities in addition to the requirements of EA Prerequisite 1 and in accordance with the LEED-NC 2009 Reference Guide:

1. Prior to the start of the construction documents phase, **designate an independent Commissioning Authority (CxA) to** lead, review and oversee the completion of all Cx process activities. The **CxA shall, at a minimum, perform tasks 2, 3 and 6.** Other team members can perform 4 & 5.

    a) CxA shall have documented CxA experience in at least 2 building projects.

    b) The individual serving as the CxA shall be:

        o   Independent of the work of design and construction

        o   Not an employee of the design firm, though may be contracted (sub) through it

        o   Not an employee of, or contracted through, a contractor or construction manager holding constr contracts

        o   Can be a qualified employee or consultant of the Owner

    c) CxA shall report results, findings and recommendations directly to the Owner.

    d) No deviation for project size in this Credit.

2. CxA shall conduct, at a **minimum, one Cx design review of the OPR, BOD and design documents prior to the mid-construction documents phase** and **back-check** the review comments in the subsequent design submission.

3. CxA shall **review contractor submittals** applicable to systems being commissioned **for compliance with the OPR and BOD**, the **review concurrent with A/E reviews and submitted to the design team and Owner.**

4. **Develop a systems manual** that provides future operating staff the information needed to understand and optimally operate the commissioned systems.

5. **Verify that the requirements for training** operating personnel and building occupants are completed.

6. **Assure** the **involve**ment by the **CxA** in review**ing building operation within 10 months after substantial completion with O&M staff and occupants**. Include a **plan for resolution of outstanding Cx-related issues**.

EA Credit 3 (cont.)

Technology and Strategy:

- Although it is preferable that the CxA be contracted by the Owner, for the enhanced commissioning credit the CxA may also be contracted through the design firms or construction management firms not holding construction contracts.
- Engage a CxA that is an independent third party.
- In addition to the requirements of EA Pr1, the CxA must review the design of all energy-related systems prior to the completion of design development.
- The CxA must review contractor submittals for all energy-related systems
- The CxA must develop or review any re-commissioning plan for energy-related systems.
- The 2009 Reference Guide provides detailed guidance as to what is expected for the following process activities:
  - Commissioning design review
  - Commissioning submittal review
  - Systems manual
- Confirm that the 6 required tasks have been completed.
- It is allowable to engage a Cx agent to conduct the design review required by EA Cr3 after construction has started as long as the project team agrees to implement any requested changes both to the documents and to construction that may have already occurred.

Calculations: na

Exemplary Performance:

- **<u>NC, Schools and C&S</u>**: Projects that conduct **comprehensive envelope Cx** may be considered for an ID credit. These projects will need to demonstrate the standards and protocol by which the envelope was commissioned.
- **<u>C&S only</u>**: consideration for ID point if the project requires the full scope of EA Pr1 and EA Cr3 for **all tenant spaces**.

Construction Submittal:

- Update the Cx plan at milestones throughout the project, at a minimum during the design development phase, construction documents phase, and just prior to the kick-off meeting with the GC.
- Prepare a systems list that indicates which systems have been included within the scope of enhanced commissioning.
- Request confirmation that the CxA has documented experience on at least 2 building projects.
- Create a written schedule of building operator trainings.
- Retain a copy of the CxA's design review, any designer responses to the review, and confirmation of the back-check.
- Retain a copy of the OPRs , BOD, Cx specifications, Cx report, and systems manual.

Timeline/Team: See EA Pr1

Regional Variations: See EA Pr1

O&M Considerations: See EA Pr1

EA Credit 4 Enhanced Refrigerant Management (2, 1, 2)

Intent: Reduce ozone depletion and support early compliance with the Montreal Protocol while minimizing direct contributions to global warming. <u>Select equipment with an efficient refrigerant charge (lbs/ton) and a long life</u>.

Option 1 – Do not use refrigerants.

Option 2 – Use Refrigerants and HVAC&R equipment that minimize or eliminate the emission of compounds that contribute to ozone depletion and global warming, **AND** do not install fire suppression systems that contain ozone-depleting substances (CFCs, HCFCs or Halons).

The base building HVAC&R equipment shall comply with the following formula which sets the maximum threshold for combined contributions to ODP and GWP:

$$LCGWP + LCODP \times 10^5 \leq 100$$

$$LCODP = [ODPr \times (Lr \times Life + Mr) \times Rc] / Life$$
$$LCGWP = [GWPr \times (Lr \times Life + Mr) \times Rc] / Life$$

LCODP:	Lifecycle ODP (lbCFC11 / Ton-Year)
LCGWP:	Lifecycle GWP (lbCO$_2$ / Ton-Year)
ODPr:	ODPr of Refrigerant (0 to 12,000 lb CO$_2$ / lb refrigerant)
GWPr:	GWPr of Refrigerant (0 to 0.2 lb CFC11 / lb refrigerant)
Lr :	Refrigerant leakage rate (0.5% to 2.0%, **default of 2%** unless otherwise demonstrated)
Mr:	End-of-life refrigerant loss (2.0% to 10%, **default of 10%** unless otherwise demonstrated)
Rc:	Refrigerant charge (0.5 to 5.0 lbs of refrigerant per ton cooling capacity)
Life:	Equipment life (10 years; **default** based on equipment type unless otherwise demonstrated): WUs **10 yrs**, DX **15 yrs**, Reciprocating compressors/Reciprocating Chillers/Scroll compressors **20 yrs**, Screw and Absorption Chillers **23 yrs**, water-cooled packaged AC units **24 yrs**, Centrifugal Chillers **25 yrs**, all others assume **15 yrs**)
ODPs:	**CFCs, HCFCs, Halons**
GWPs:	**CFCs, HCFCs, HFCs**

For multiple types of equipment, use a <u>weighted average</u> of all base building level HVACR equipment <u>gross ARI rated tons</u>. **Values other than default values** may be used if approved by USGBC; if not yet approved, submit the following at a minimum:
>Manufacturer's test data for annual leakage rates
>Refrigerant leak detection equipment in the room where the equipment is located
>Preventative maintenance program for minimizing leakage
>Program for recovering and recycling refrigerant at the end of equipment life

Small **HVAC units**, defined as **containing <u>less than 0.5 lbs</u> of refrigerant**, and other equipment **such as standard refrigerators**, small water coolers, and any other cooling that contains less than 0.5 lbs of refrigerant, are not considered part of the "base building" system and **are not subject to the requirements of this credit.**

If the building is connected to an existing CHW system, the CHW supplier must perform the required calculations and submit a letter showing compliance.

"Natural refrigerants", e.g. H$_2$O, CO$_2$ and NH$_4$, have much lower ODP and GWP.

The Clean Air Act, Section 608, requires the following to minimize refrigerant leakage:

- Recycle ODPs during servicing and disposal of AC&R equipment.
- Set certification requirements for refrigerant recycling/recovery equipment, technicians, reclaimers and buyers.
- Persons servicing/disposing AC&R equipment must certify to EPA they use recycling/recovery equipment and obey the rule.
- Repair substantial leaks in AC&R equipment with a charge of greater than 50 pounds.
- Establish safe disposal requirements for removal of refrigerants from goods that enter waste streams with charge intact.
- Never knowingly vent ozone-depleting compounds used as refrigerants while working with AC&R equipment.

The Montreal Protocol originally called for all CFCs and HCFCs to be phased out by 2030.

Following a proposal and strong endorsement by the United States, the 191 Parties to the Montreal Protocol reached an historic agreement to accelerate efforts to ensure recovery of the stratospheric ozone layer at a meeting in Montreal that concluded Friday, September 21, 2007. The **Parties agreed to <u>speed up by a decade</u> the phase-out of hydrochlorofluorocarbons (HCFCs)**.

- Developing countries will push forward setting their baseline for production and consumption of HCFCs from 2015 to 2009-2010.
- Developing countries will also freeze production and consumption of HCFCs in 2013 instead of 2016.
- **Developed countries will <u>phase out production of HCFCs by 2020</u>.**
- **Developed countries will reduce HCFC consumption by 75% in 2010, 90% in 2015 with a <u>phase out in 2020</u>.**
- Developing countries will reduce their HCFC production and consumption by 10% in 2015, by 35% in 2020, by 67.5% in 2025 with a phase-out in 2030.

The following shows the ODP and direct GWP of common HCFC and HFC refrigerants. Note that **although HFCs have an ODP that is essentially zero, HFCs are slightly less efficient than HCFCs** and the **GWPs of HFCs are substantially higher than some of the HCFCs**.

Refrigerant	ODP	GWP	Applications
HCFC-22	0.04	1,780	Air conditioning, chillers
HCFC-123	0.02	76	CFC-11 replacement
HFC-23	approx. 0	12,240	Ultra-low-temp refrigeration
HFC-134a	**approx. 0**	**1,320**	CFC-12 or HCFC-22 replacement
HFC-245fa	approx. 0	1,020	Insulation agent, centrifugal chillers
HFC-404A	approx. 0	3,900	Low-temp refrigeration
HFC-407C	**approx. 0**	**1,700**	HCFC-22 replacement
HFC-410A	**approx. 0**	**1,890**	Air conditioning
HFC-507A	approx. 0	3,900	Low-temp refrigeration

Technology and Strategy:

- Do not use refrigerants.
- Use only natural refrigerants.
- Select refrigerants with low ODP and GWP.
- Minimize refrigerant leakage.
- Select equipment with efficient refrigerant charge.
- Select equipment with long service life.
- Select alternative fire-suppression systems.

Calculations: use refrigerant charge, refrigerant life, equipment type, and the formulas above

Default Maximum Allowable Refrigerant Charge (lb/ton) for EA Cr4 Compliance (**1-2% higher for Centrifugals**)

Refrigerant	PTAC (10 yr)	Split/Pkg DX (15 yr)	Recip/Scroll CHs (20 yr)	Screw/Absorp CHs (23 yr)
R-22	0.57	0.64	0.69	0.71
R-123	1.60	1.80	1.92	1.97
R-134a	2.52	2.80	3.03	3.10
R-407c	1.95	2.20	2.35	2.41
R-410a	1.76	1.98	2.11	2.17

Exemplary Performance: na

Design submittal: Use Submittal Templates
- Provide HVAC&R equipment types including number, size, refrigerant type, refrigerant charge and life.
- Narrative describing any special circumstances or calculation explanations.

Timeline/Team: Consult with Mechanical Engineer or HVAC specialist during design phase.

Regional Variations: na
O&M Considerations: See EA Prerequisite 3.

EA Credit 5 Measurement and Verification (3, 2, 0)

Intent (<u>for NC and Schools only</u>): Provide for the ongoing accountability of building energy consumption over time.

Requirements:

OPTION 1:

- Develop and implement an M&V plan consistent with **<u>Option D: Calibrated Simulation</u>** (Savings Estimation Method 2), as specified in the ***International Performance Measurement & Verification Protocol (IPMVP) Volume III****: Concepts and Options for Determining Energy Savings in New Construction, April 2003.*
- The M&V period <u>shall cover a period of at least one year of post-construction occupancy</u>.
- Provide a <u>process for corrective action</u> if the results of the M&V plan indicate that energy savings are not being achieved.

OPTION 2:

- Develop and implement an M&V plan consistent with **<u>Option B: Energy Conservation Measure Isolation</u>**, as specified in the ***International Performance Measurement & Verification Protocol (IPMVP) Volume III****: Concepts and Options for Determining Energy Savings in New Construction, April 2003.*
- The M&V period <u>shall cover a period of at least one year of post-construction occupancy</u>.
- Provide a <u>process for corrective action</u> if the results of the M&V plan indicate that energy savings are not being achieved.

Option 1 – Calibrated Simulation:
- Most suited **for buildings with large number of ECMs or interactive systems**.
- Isolation and measurement and verification (M&V) of individual ECMs is impractical or inappropriate.
- <u>Use a computer model</u> to compare actual energy use to calibrated computer model (<u>from EA Cr1 Opt 1</u>).

Option 2 – Energy Conservation Measure Isolation:

- Most suited **for smaller and/or simpler buildings**.
- Isolate the main energy systems and apply Option B to each system on an individual basis.
- <u>May also need to implement whole-building metering/tracking to satisfy the intent of this credit</u>.

Technology and Strategy:

- Develop an M&V Plan to evaluate building and/or energy system performance.
- Characterize the building and/or energy systems through energy simulation or engineering analysis.
- Install the necessary metering equipment to measure energy use.
- Track performance by comparing predicted to actual performance, by component or system as appropriate.
- Use IPMVP guidance to use M&V activities for situations other than ECMs to provide for ongoing building analysis.
- For the corrective action process, consider installing diagnostics within the control system to alert staff that equipment is not being optimally operated. Alarms to alert staff should include:
    - Leaking valves in the cooling and heating coils within AHUs
    - Missed economizer opportunities (e.g. faulty economizer damper controls)
    - Software and manual overrides allowing equipment to operate 24/7
    - Equipment operation during unusual circumstances (e.g. boiler on when OAT above 65 degrees)
- Consider hiring retro-commissioning service companies or dedicating staff to investigate high energy bills.

Calculations: use IPMVP Vol. III formulae and guidelines
Exemplary Performance: na
Construction Submittal

Timeline/Team: See Table 3 in the GBC&C Reference Guide.

Regional Variations: Not applicable for methodology, but there are some regional variations for climate.

O&M Considerations: Consider sub-metering major energy end uses to help operators identify deviations from expected use.

EA Credit 5.1 Measurement and Verification – Base Building (0, 0, 3)

Intent (Core & Shell only): Provide for the ongoing accountability of building energy consumption over time.

Requirements:

OPTION 1:

- Develop and implement an M&V plan consistent with **Option D: Calibrated Simulation** (Savings Estimation Method 2), as specified in the ***International Performance Measurement & Verification Protocol (IPMVP) Volume III****: Concepts and Options for Determining Energy Savings in New Construction, April 2003.*
- The documentation must include the following:
    o   A description of the infrastructure design.
    o   Existing meter locations.
    o   Existing meter specifications
    o   1-line electrical schematics identifying end-use circuits.
    o   Guidelines for carrying out tenant sub-metering.

OPTION 2:

- Develop and implement an M&V plan consistent with **Option B: Energy Conservation Measure Isolation**, as specified in the ***International Performance Measurement & Verification Protocol (IPMVP) Volume III****: Concepts and Options for Determining Energy Savings in New Construction, April 2003.*
- The documentation must include the following:
    o   A description of the infrastructure design.
    o   Existing meter locations.
    o   Existing meter specifications
    o   1-line electrical schematics identifying end-use circuits.
    o   Guidelines for carrying out tenant sub-metering.

- This credit focuses on the energy-using systems of the C&S building (primarily electric-using systems) and may include measuring electricity in the tenant spaces.
- For the purposes of this credit, the electricity use of the tenant spaces does not have to be itemized by the tenant.
- The M&V plan should address the electricity-using systems in the C&S building.
- Infrastructure, e.g. meters or a building management system, must be provided.
- The building is not eligible if it does not have any electricity-using systems.

EA Credit 5.2 Measurement and Verification – Tenant Submetering (0, 0, 3)

Intent (Core & Shell only): Provide for the ongoing accountability of building electricity consumption over time.
Requirements:
- Include a **centrally monitored electronic metering network in the base building design** that is capable of being expanded to accommodate the future tenant sub-metering **as required by LEED for Commercial Interiors 2009 EA Cr3: M&V**.
- Develop **a tenant M&V plan** that documents and advises future tenants of this opportunity and the means of achievement.
- Provide a **process for corrective action** if the results of the M&V plan indicate that energy savings are not being achieved.

Submetering:
- The **goal** of submetering is to give tenants an **incentive to save energy**.
- It allows tenants to **see a return** on any conservation investments they make.
- It gives tenants the **opportunity** to realize savings by reducing energy use or implementing energy efficiency measures.
- Submeters are **not a major expense**.
- **Some** utilities **do not allow a second party to charge** for electricity based on submetering; in this case, provide **separate meters** for each tenant **or**, for buildings with submeters, cost can be **apportion**ed **based on usage**.

EA Credit 6 Green Power (2, 2, 2)

Intent: Encourage the development and use of grid-source, renewable energy technologies on a net zero pollution basis.
Requirements:

- Engage in **at least a 2-year renewable energy contract** to provide **at least 35%** of the building's **electricity from renewable sources**, as **defined by the Center for Resource Solutions (CRS) Green-e Energy products certification requirements**.
- **All purchases of green power shall be <u>based on the quantity of energy consumed, not cost</u>.**

Schools (additional): School districts can purchase green power on a centralized basis and allocate the green power to a specific project. However, the same power cannot be credited to another LEED project. Submit a letter from the company owner attesting to this.

Core & Shell (additional): The C&S building's electricity is defined as the electricity usage of the C&S square footage, as defined by the Building Owners and Managers Association (**BOMA**) Standards, but not less than 15% of the building total gross square footage.

OPTION 1 - <u>DETERMINE</u> BASELINE ELECTRICITY USE:
Use the annual electricity consumption from the results of <u>EA Cr1</u>

OPTION 2 - <u>ESTIMATE</u> BASELINE ELECTRICITY USE:
Use the DOE's Commercial Buildings Energy Consumption Survey (<u>CBECS</u>) to determine the estimated electricity consumption.

Note:
There are **3 approaches for achieving this credit**:

1. **In a state with an open electrical market**, the <u>Owners may have the ability to select</u> a Green-e Energy certified <u>power provider from which to purchase at least 35%</u> of their annual electrical power.
2. **In a state with a closed electrical market**, the <u>Governing Utility Company may have</u> a Green-e Energy certified utility <u>program in which Owners can enroll for at least 35%</u> of the provided electrical energy, **usually at a premium.**
3. **If direct purchase is not available through local utilities**, the <u>Owner and Project Team have the option of purchasing</u> accredited **Renewable Energy Certificates (RECs), or "Green Tags"**, <u>equal to at least 35%</u> of the predicted annual electrical consumption over a 2-year period (i.e. a <u>one-time purchase every 2 years equivalent to 70% of the **predicted annual electrical consumption</u>**). **TRCs are Tradable Renewable Certificates.**

Establishing Green-e Equivalency: The <u>power product purchased</u> to comply with the credit requirements <u>need not be Green-e Energy certified</u>, <u>but</u> projects are **required to document to the USGBC** that the <u>renewable supplier has</u> (1) <u>met the current Green-e Energy Standard</u>, and (2) <u>properly accounted</u> for the eligible renewable resources sold (the renewable energy supplier must have undergone an independent 3rd party verification that the standard has been met; the 3rd party verification process must be as rigorous as that used in the Green-e certification process and must be performed annually).

For <u>renewable energy</u> from both on-site and off-site sources, the associated environmental attributes must be retained or retired; they cannot be sold.

Technology and Strategy:

- **Green Power** - Derive green power from solar, wind, geothermal, biomass or low-impact hydro sources.
- **Non Green-e Energy Certified Power** – RECs, TRCs, Green Tags and other sources of green power that comply with Green-e Energy program's technical requirements can be used to document compliance with EA Cr6.

Calculations: use EA Cr1 simulation calculations or DOE database (CBECS).
Exemplary Performance: Purchase 100% of electricity from renewable sources.
Construction Submittal

Timeline/Team: Project team should estimate the potential use of the building during the design phase.

Regional Variations: RECs are available in most states; customers can buy them even if they don't have access to green power through their local utility or a competitive electricity marketer.
O&M Considerations: Give building operators details on the original contract to facilitate renewal beyond 2 years.

Materials and Resources (MR) NC 8-14 Pts, Schools 8-13 Pts, C&S 6-13 Pts

Achieving LEED MR credits can reduce the quantity of waste while improving the building environment through responsible waste management and materials.

MR credits focus on 2 main issues:
- The environmental impact of materials brought into the project building
- The minimization of landfill and incinerator disposal for materials that leave the project building.

MR credits address the environmental concerns related to materials selection, waste disposal and waste reduction as follows:

Select Sustainable Materials
- Material extraction, processing, transportation, use, and disposal can affect water, air, native habitats and natural resources.
- Select materials with recycled content and materials from local sources.

Practice Waste Reduction
- Construction and demolition wastes constitute about 40% of the total solid waste stream in the US.
- The EPA ranks **source reduction**, **reuse** and **recycling** as the 3 preferred strategies for reducing waste.

Reduce Waste at Its Source
- **Source reduction**, including reducing the overall demand for products, **is the most economical way to reduce waste**.
- In 2006, US residents, businesses and institutions produced over 251 million tons of solid waste, 65% above 1980 levels.
- This is equal to 4.6 pounds per day per person, 25% above 1980 levels.
- Total municipal solid waste generation in 2006 was 34% paper/cardboard, 13% yard trimmings and 12% food scraps.
- In addition, 7.6 billion tons of industrial solid waste are generated year.
- Unnecessary materials (e.g. packaging) add to product cost, and fees for waste collection/disposal rise as waste increases.

Reuse and Recycling
- Specify reuse of interior components in the construction documents.
- Salvaged materials can be substituted for new materials
- Recycled-content materials reuse waste otherwise disposed of in landfills or incinerators.
- Rapidly renewable materials may minimize natural resource consumption.
- Use of 3rd party certified wood improves the stewardship of forests and related ecosystems.
- Recycling waste has increased in the US from 6.4% in 1960 to 32.5% in 2006.
- Recycling avoids the use of virgin materials, avoids raw material extraction and preserves landfill space.
- Recycling can prevent toxic materials from polluting the air and ground water.
- Reuse and recycling can save money by reducing disposal costs and generating revenue from recycling or resale.

Calculating Materials Costs
- Actual: use Construction Specification Institute (**CSI**) **MasterFormat Division 03-10, 31 and 32**, excluding labor and eqpt.
- Estimated: assume 45% of the total construction costs, including labor and eqpt., using Divisions 03-10, 31 and 32.
- Note: Use the 45% estimate if the actual material cost is > 45%.
- Material costs from **MasterFormat Division 12 – Furniture and Furnishings** may be included as long as this is done consistently across all MR credits.
- Core & Shell project teams that use tenant sales or lease agreements to assist with credit compliance must also do so consistently across all MR credits.
- **Materials calculated toward materials reuse cannot be applied to MR credits for building reuse, construction waste management, recycled content, rapidly renewable materials or certified wood**.

Soft costs include Architect fees, Engineer fees, financing costs and legal fees.

MR Prerequisite 1 Storage and Collection of Recyclables

Intent: Facilitate the reduction of waste generated by building occupants that is hauled to and disposed of in landfills.

Requirements:

- Provide an easily accessible dedicated area for the collection and storage of materials for recycling for the entire building.
- Materials must include at a minimum paper, corrugated cardboard, glass, plastics and metals.

Although the requirements of this prerequisite do not regulate the size of the recycling area, the following table provides guidelines for the recycling storage area based on overall building area.

Commercial Building Area (ft^2)	Minimum Recycling Area (ft^2)
0 to 5,000	82
5,001 to 15,000	125
15,001 to 50,000	175
50,001 to 100,000	225
100,001 to 200,000	275
200,001 or greater	500

Recycle 1 ton of paper: saves 17 trees and 3 cubic yards of landfill
Recycled Aluminum: requires 5% of the energy required to produce Aluminum from bauxite

Implementation:

- Designate an area for recyclable collection and storage that is appropriately sized and located in a convenient area.
- Identify local waste handlers and buyers for glass, plastic, office paper, newspaper, cardboard and organic wastes.
- Instruct occupants on recycling procedures.
- Consider employing cardboard balers, aluminum can crushers, recycling chutes and other waste strategies.

Calculations: na

Exemplary Performance: na

Design Submittal

Timeline/Team:
- Early in the design phase, seek input from local haulers.
- Prior to occupancy, the owner should ensure that sufficient recycling bins are in place.
- After occupancy, the project should educate occupants and facilities.

Regional Variations: Research local recycling programs.

O&M Considerations: Consider developing a commercial waste and recycling policy and education program for occupants; the policy should outline protocol and signage; the education program should explain the environmental and financial benefits of recycling.

MR Credit 1/1.1 Building Reuse: Maintain Existing Walls, Floors and Roof (1-3, 1-2, 1-5)

<u>Note: (This Credit is called MR Credit 1 for Core & Shell because there is no MR Credit 1.2 for Core & Shell)</u>

Intent: Extend the life cycle of existing building stock, conserve resources, retain cultural resources, reduce waste and reduce environmental impacts of new buildings as they relate to materials manufacturing and transport.

Requirements:
- Maintain the existing building's:
    - **structure** (including structural floor and roof decking)
    - **envelope** (exterior skin and framing, excluding windows, doors and non-structural roofing material)
- Hazardous materials that are remediated as part of the project scope must be excluded from calculation of the % maintained.
- <u>Not applicable if</u> the square footage of a building <u>addition is more than 2 times the square footage of the existing building</u>.

Points for building reuse are awarded for achieving the following levels of reuse:

New Construction	**Schools**	**Core & Shell**
55% reuse: 1 point	75% reuse: 1 point	25% reuse: 1 point
75% reuse: 2 points	95% reuse: 2 points	33% reuse: 2 points
95% reuse: 3 points		42% reuse: 3 points
		50% reuse: 4 points
		75% reuse: 5 points

Develop floor plans showing the following:

- Structural components
- Exterior and **party walls** (walls that are shared by two adjoining buildings)
- Exterior windows and doors
- Hazardous or unsound structural or envelope components

Structural support elements (<u>columns and beams</u>) are "part of the larger surfaces they support", i.e. <u>not quantified separately</u>.

Projects that are incorporating <u>existing buildings but can't get credit for MR Cr1</u> can <u>apply</u> the reused <u>lbs</u> towards <u>MR Cr2</u>.

Implementation:

- Consider the reuse of existing, previously occupied buildings including the structure, envelope and elements.
- Remove elements that pose contamination risk to building occupants.
- Upgrade components that would improve energy and water efficiency, e.g. windows, mechanical systems and plumbing fixtures.

Calculations:

- **Structural floors and roof decking:** calculate the square footage of each component.
- **Exterior walls:** use <u>1 side</u> only, **subtract windows and doors** for the existing and reused areas.
- **Interior walls:** structural walls only, e.g. shear walls, **<u>use 1 side</u>**, subtract doors and other openings.
- Exclude: non-structural roofing material, windows, and unsound or hazardous materials.

Exemplary Performance (<u>C&S only</u>): maintain 95% or more of the existing walls, floors and roof.

Construction Submittal

Timeline/Team: Impacts all phases of the project.

Regional Variations: Consider historic structures/neighborhoods, inner city investments, and areas where there is pressure to demolish existing structures and build larger buildings.

O&M Considerations: Notify building operators of special maintenance practices, or reduction in lifespan or durability vs new.

MR Credit 1.2 Building Reuse: Maintain Interior Non-Structural Elements (1, 1, 0)

Intent (for NC and Schools only): Extend the life cycle of existing building stock, conserve resources, retain cultural resources, reduce waste and reduce environmental impacts of new buildings as they relate to materials manufacturing and transport.

Requirements:

- Use existing **interior non-structural elements** (interior walls, doors, floor coverings and ceiling systems) in **at least 50% by area** of the total area of the completed building, including additions.
- Not applicable if the square footage of a building addition is more than 2 times the square footage of the existing building.

Develop floor plans showing the following:

- Finish ceilings and flooring
- Interior walls (differentiate between shear and non-shear)
- Doors within interior walls
- Built-in casework to be reused

Fixed items, e.g. walls and doors, can be counted if used for the same purpose. If different purpose, use MR Cr 3.1 & 3.2.

Projects that are incorporating existing buildings but can't get credit for MR Cr1 can apply the reused lbs towards MR Cr2.

Implementation:

- Consider the reuse of existing buildings, including the structure, envelope and interior non-structural elements.
- Remove elements that pose contamination risk to building occupants.
- Upgrade components that would improve energy and water efficiency.
- Quantify the extent of building reuse.

Calculations:

- Finished floors and ceilings: calculate as one sided.
- Interior non-structural walls: use 2 sides from floor to ceiling only, count 1 side of doors.
- Interior Casework: calculate using the visible surface area of the assembly.
- Exterior structural and party walls: if the interior finishes have been used, count 1 side.

Exemplary Performance: na

Construction Submittal

Timeline/Team: Impacts all phases of the project. Architectural drawings should provide the detail needed to determine the surface area of all reused elements.

Regional Variations: Consider local historical context and constrained landfill space.

O&M Considerations: Notify building operators of special maintenance practices, or reduction in lifespan or durability for the reused material.

MR Credit 2 Construction Waste Management (1-2, 1-2, 1-2)

Intent:

- Divert construction and demolition debris from disposal in landfills and incineration facilities.
- Redirect recyclable recovered resources back to the manufacturing process.
- Redirect reusable materials to appropriate sites.

Requirements:

- Recycle and/or salvage at least **50% (1 point) or 75% (2 points)** of non-hazardous construction and demolition debris.
- Develop and implement a construction waste management plan that at a minimum:
    - Identifies the materials to be diverted from disposal
    - States whether the materials will be sorted on-site or co-mingled
- Not applicable to excavated soil, land-clearing debris or hazardous waste.
- Applicable to crushed and reused existing concrete, masonry or asphalt - if they are crushed and reused on-site.
- Applies to construction debris processed into a recycled content commodity that has an open market value.
- Calculations can be done **by weight or volume**, but must be **consistent throughout**.

The greatest environmental benefit is achieved by source control, i.e. reducing the total waste generated.

GENERAL CONTRACTOR MUST PROVIDE DATA AND DOCUMENTATION

Implementation:

- Establish goals for diversion from disposal in landfills and incineration facilities.
- Adopt a construction waste management plan to achieve these goals.
- Consider recycling cardboard, metal, brick, mineral fiber panel, concrete, plastic, clean wood, glass, gypsum wallboard, carpet and insulation.
- Construction debris processed into a recycled content commodity which has an open market value - e.g. Wood Derived Fuel (WDF), alternative daily cover material, etc. – may be applied to the construction waste calculation.
- Designate a specific area(s) on the construction site for segregated or commingled collection of recycled materials.
- Track recycling efforts throughout the construction process.
- Identify construction haulers and recyclers to handle the designated materials.
- Note that diversion may include donation of materials to charitable organizations and salvage of materials on-site. Materials **salvaged and reused on-site can contribute** to this credit **if they are not included in MR Credit 3**.

Calculations:

- Divide the amount of waste diverted by the total generated on-site (use weight or volume, but be consistent throughout)

Exemplary Performance: Divert 95%

Construction Submittal

Timeline/Team: Create Plan during the Design Phase; **GC** should identify recycling locations and requirements; during construction, the **GC** should confirm that the Plan is implemented, track waste and report to the project team; after construction, **GC** should complete documentation and submit detailed records to the team.

Regional Variations: Some materials, e.g. drywall, can only be recycled if there is a processing plant or if the soil can handle it; demolished materials may need to be taken apart, e.g. take nails out of wood; distance to recycling centers in rural or remote areas may outweigh benefits; landfill space, waste diversion options or tipping fees should be considered.

O&M Considerations: The challenge is to identify appropriate receivers for waste; **GCs** should develop a company policy and educate employees.

MR Credit 3 Materials Reuse (1-2, 1-2, 1)

Intent: Reuse building materials and products in order to <u>reduce demand</u> for virgin materials <u>and</u> to <u>reduce waste</u>, thereby reducing impacts associated with the <u>extraction</u> <u>and</u> <u>processing</u> of <u>virgin resources</u>.

Requirements:

- Use **salvaged, refurbished or reused materials**.
- <u>**C&S**</u>: the sum of these materials must be at least **5% (1 point)**, **based on cost**, of the total value **of materials** on the project.
- <u>**NC and Schools only**</u>: the sum of these materials must be at least **5% (1 point) or 10% (2 points)**, **based on cost**, of the total value **of materials** on the project.
- **No M/E/P components or specialty equipment**, e.g. elevator equipment, shall be included in the calculations.
- **Only permanently installed materials** shall be included.
- **Furniture and furnishings (CSI Division 12 components) may be included if included consistently in MR Credits 3-7**.

Note: This credit applies primarily to CSI MasterFormat 2004 03-10, 31 and 32. For salvaged furniture taken from the occupant's previous location/facility, the items must have been purchased 2 years prior to the project initiation.

Reuse of Fixed Materials: on-site before the project started, no longer able to serve original function, reconditioned for use in the project, and installed for a different use or in a different location (e.g. door converted to a countertop).

Reuse of Finish Materials: kept and refurbished, able to serve original function only after refurbishment (e.g. door knob)

Reuse of Off-site Materials: must have been previously used, don't have to be from a building i.e. can be purchased as salvage or relocated from another facility (<u>salvage from both on-site and off-site may be applied toward MR Credit 5: Regional Materials</u>).

<u>Materials</u> contributing toward <u>achieving Credit 3</u> <u>cannot</u> be applied to <u>Credits 1, 2, 4, 6 or 7</u>.

If Credit 3 is not being attempted, applicable materials may be applied toward another Credit if eligible.

Buildings account for 40% of the raw stone, gravel and sand, as well as 25% of virgin wood, of natural resources consumed.

Implementation:

- Identify opportunities to incorporate salvaged materials into building design.
- Research potential material suppliers.
- Consider salvaged materials such as beams and posts, flooring, paneling, doors and frames, cabinetry and furniture, brick and decorative items.
- Do not include materials containing hazardous materials, e.g. lead or asbestos.

Calculations:

- Use the <u>highest of</u> either <u>Actual</u> Item Cost <u>or</u> <u>Equivalent New</u> Item Cost for reused or salvaged items.
- May use <u>default total material cost at 45% of Total Construction Cost</u>, <u>especially if actual</u> material cost <u>is > 45%</u>.
- Conversely, it is better to use actual cost if the actual cost is < 45% of the Total Construction Cost.

Exemplary Performance: <u>NC and Schools</u> reuse 15%; **<u>C&S</u>** reuse 10%.

Construction Submittal

Timeline/Team: Design – Start early in the Pre-design phase with Owner, Architect and Contractor; **Contractor** should locate sources and document/track material costs and quantities.

Regional Variations: Important for historic structures or neighborhoods; New England, Pacific NW and California have well-developed markets for salvaged material
O&M Considerations: na

MR Credit 4 Recycled Content (1-2, 1-2, 1-2)

Intent: Increase demand for building products that incorporate recycled content materials, thereby reducing impacts resulting from extraction and processing of virgin materials.

Requirements:

- Sum(post-consumer recycled content cost + ½ of the pre-consumer recycled content cost) =
    at least **10% (1 point) or 20% (2 points)** of Total Material Cost
- For each material/product, use **(% by lbs)** x (material or product $) to determine Post- and/or Pre-consumer cost.
- Recycled content value of a material assembly is determined by **% of assembly weight (lbs) x assembly cost**.
- No M/E/P components or specialty equipment, e.g. elevator equipment and appliances, shall be included in the calculations.
- Only permanently installed materials shall be included.
- Furniture and furnishings may be included, provided it is included consistently in MR Credits 3-7.
- Recycled content shall be defined in accordance with International Organization for Standards document *ISO 14021 – 1999 Environmental Labels and Declarations – Self-declared Environmental Claims (Type II environmental labeling)*.

Post-Consumer Content Materials:

- Waste material **generated by households or facilities in their role as end-users of the product**
- The product can **no longer be used for its intended purpose**.
- Examples: construction/demolition debris, curbside and drop-off recyclables, broken refurbished pallets (not new), discarded products (furniture, cabinets, decking), and urban maintenance waste (leaves, grass clippings, tree trimmings, etc.).

Pre-Consumer Content Materials:

- Waste material **diverted from the waste stream during the manufacturing process**
- Not applicable to reutilization of rework, regrind or scrap generated in a process and capable of being reclaimed within the same process that generated it because this waste would not normally be hauled off as garbage.
- Examples of pre-consumer content materials: planer shavings, plytrim, sawdust, chips, bagasse, sunflower seed hulls, walnut shells, culls, trimmed materials, print overruns, over-issue publications, obsolete inventories.

Assembly Recycled Content:

- Assemblies include all products composed of multiple materials.
- The materials are composed either in a formulation (composite wood panels) or as sub-components (window system).
- Pre- and/or Post-consumer content cost is determined by % of assembly weight (lbs) x assembly total cost.

Supplementary Cementitious Materials (SCMs):

- For **SCMs** used in concrete that are recycled from other operations, base the recycled content value on the weight of the cementitious materials only, rather than on the entire concrete mix, e.g. **fly ash (pre-consumer)**.

Exclude M/E/P Components and Specialty Equipment:

- Exclude M/E/P components, appliances and equipment form the calculations.
- Mechanical and electric equipment tends to have a high dollar value relative to the amount of material it contains.
- The high dollar value would skew the calculations and reduce the incentive to use recycled content in high-mass materials.

Implementation:

- Establish a project goal for recycled content materials and identify material suppliers that can achieve this goal.
- During construction, ensure that the specified recycled content materials are installed.
- Consider a range of environmental, economic and performance attributes when selecting products and materials.

MR Credit 4 (cont.)

Calculations:

- Use **CSI MasterFormat** 2004 Divisions 03-10, 31 and 32.
- List the recycled content materials/products used in the project and the cost for each.
- For each material or product, calculate % by lbs to determine Post- and/or Pre-consumer cost.
- Sum [Post-consumer cost + ½(pre-consumer cost)] / [Total Project Material Cost].
- May <u>use default</u> total material cost at <u>45% of Total Construction Cost, especially if actual material cost is > 45%</u>.
- May <u>use default steel</u> recycled content at <u>25% post-consumer</u>, although **many steel products are ≥ 90% recycled**.

Contractor should run preliminary calculations during the preconstruction phase whenever possible.

Exemplary Performance: recycle 30%

Construction Submittal

Timeline/Team: Run preliminary calculations during the design phase to set recycled content targets; consult with suppliers; Architect should identify and specify products; **Contractor** should ensure appropriate installation, documenting and tracking costs and quantities of recycled materials, and providing the documentation to the project team.

Regional Variations: Location affects availability of locally sourced materials; the Project Team must decide between local virgin materials or recycled material imported from a long distance.

O&M Considerations: Recycled materials may require different maintenance requirements than conventional products; encourage a sustainable purchasing plan and provide building operators with a list of installed products and their manufacturers.

MR Credit 5 Regional Materials (1-2, 1-2, 1-2)

Intent: Increase demand for building materials and products that are extracted and manufactured within the region, thereby supporting the use of indigenous resources and reducing the environmental impacts resulting from transportation.

Requirements:

- Use materials that have been **extracted, harvested, recovered or manufactured <u>within 500 miles</u>** of the site.
- Minimum of **10% (1 point) or 20% (2 points), based on cost**, of the Total Material Cost.
- **Use % by weight** for fractions of materials/products that are "regional".
- **No M/E/P components or specialty equipment**, e.g. elevator equipment, shall be included in the calculations.
- Only permanently installed materials shall be included.
- <u>Furniture and furnishings may be included</u>, provided it is included consistently in MR Credits 3-7.

Point of Extraction: where the material is salvaged
Point of Manufacturing: where the material is bought, i.e. vendor location

GENERAL CONTRACTOR SHOULD PERFORM THE FOLLOWING:

- Work with subs and suppliers to verify availability of the materials
- Run preliminary budget calculations during the preconstruction phase to focus on regional materials
- Document the distance, amount and value for each regional material

Implementation:

- Run <u>preliminary calculations during the Design Phase.</u>
- Establish a project goal for locally sourced materials and identify material suppliers that can achieve this goal.
- During construction, ensure that the specified local materials are installed and quantify the percentage.
- Consider a range of environmental, economic and performance attributes when selecting products and materials.
- **Reused and salvaged materials that satisfy <u>MR Cr 3.1 and 3.2</u> may also contribute to MR Cr 5.1 and 5.2.**

Calculations:

- Use CSI MasterFormat 2004 Divisions 03-10, 31 and 32.
- List the local materials/products used in the project and the cost for each.
- For fractions that are local, for each material/product calculate % by lbs to determine local fractional cost.
- Sum the local material/product costs and divide by the Total Project Material Cost.
- May <u>use default</u> total material cost at <u>45% of Total Construction Cost, especially if actual material cost is > 45%</u>.

Exemplary Performance: Use 30% regional materials.

Construction Submittal

Timeline/Team: Architect should specify regional materials; during construction, the **GC** should document amounts and values of regional materials; the **GC** must track the materials cost.

Regional Variations: Availability will vary by regions; consider local design aesthetics, stability of local materials in the local climate, and local architecture.

O&M Considerations: Maintain information on the installed products; encourage sustainable purchasing plan and provide building operators with a list of the installed products and their manufacturers.

MR Credit 6 Rapidly Renewable Materials (1, 1, 0)

Intent <u>(for NC and Schools only)</u>: Reduce the use and depletion of finite raw materials and long-cycle renewable materials by replacing them with rapidly renewable materials.

Requirements:

- Use rapidly renewable materials/products, i.e. made from plants **harvested within a 10 year or shorter cycle**.
- Use rapidly renewable materials/products worth at least **2.5%, based on cost**, of the Total Material Cost.

Examples: bamboo, wool, cotton, agrifiber, linoleum, wheatboard, strawbales, cork, bio-based paints, geotextile fabrics such as coir and jute, and natural rubber

Embodied Energy: energy used during the entire life cycle of a product, including its' manufacture, transportation and disposal, and the inherent energy captured within the product itself.

Implementation:

- Project Team should run preliminary calculations during the Design Phase.
- Establish a project goal for rapidly renewable materials and identify products and vendors that can achieve this goal.

Calculations:

- Use CSI MasterFormat 2004 Divisions 03-10, 31 and 32.
- List the renewable materials/products used in the project and the cost for each.
- For assemblies, for each material/product calculate **% by lbs** to determine renewable fraction cost.
- Sum the renewable material/product costs and divide by the Total Project Material Cost.
- May <u>use default</u> total material cost at 45% of Total Construction Cost, <u>especially if actual material cost is > 45%</u>.

Exemplary Performance: use 5% rapidly renewable materials/products.

Construction Submittal

Timeline/Team: Architect should specify rapidly renewable materials; during construction, the **GC** should ensure proper installation and collect product documentation.

Regional Variations: Availability will vary by regions; consider availability of rapidly renewable materials that also contribute to MR Cr5 (within 500 miles).

O&M Considerations: Address special maintenance practices, e.g. bamboo and cork exposure to excessive moisture; obtain data from the manufacturer and give it to the building operators.

MR Credit 6/7 Certified Wood (1, 1, 1)

Note: (This Credit is called MR Credit 6 for Core & Shell because there is no MR Credit 7 for Core & Shell)

Intent (for NC and Schools only): Encourage environmentally responsible forest management.

Requirements:

- For wood building components, use a minimum of **50%, based on cost**, of wood-based materials and products that are certified in accordance with the Forest Stewardship Council's principles and criteria.
- These components include at a minimum structural framing and general dimensional framing, flooring, sub-flooring, wood doors and finishes.
- Only permanently installed materials are included, except for bracing, forming, scaffolding, sidewalk protection, and guardrails
- If any temporary materials are included, then all temporary materials must be included, and only for one Project.
- Furniture and furnishings may be included, provided it is included consistently in MR Credits 3-7.

Forest Stewardship Council (FSC):

- The FSC ensures that forestry practices are environmentally responsible, socially beneficial and economically viable.
- Environmental perspective: sustainable timber harvesting, preserving wildlife habitat and biodiversity, maintaining soil and water quality, minimizing the use of harmful chemicals, and conserving forests of high conservation value.
- As of 2007, FSC forests represented 7% of the world's productive forests.
- Economic perspective: current costs for FSC-certified wood products are equal to or higher than conventional wood products, and availability varies by region; prices are expected to become more competitive.
- The FSC accredits and monitors certification organizations; uses independent 3rd-party auditors qualified to annually evaluate compliance with FSC standards on the ground and to award **2 types of Certifications**.
- The majority of FSC certification audits in North America are by SmartWood and Scientific Certification Systems.

Forest Management Certification:

- Awarded to responsible forest managers after **successful completion of audits of forestry practices and plans**.
- Awarded to forest managers who adopt environmentally and socially responsible forest management practices.

Chain of Custody Certification:

- Chain of Custody (COC) is a tracking procedure for a product from the point of harvest or extraction to its end use.
- COC Certification is awarded to companies that process, manufacture and/or sell products made of certified wood.
- The COC certificate number is listed on invoices of non-labeled products to document that an entity has followed FSC guidelines for product accounting.
- COC certification is awarded based on **successful completion of audits** to ensure the following:
    - o proper use of the FSC name and logo
    - o segregation of certified and noncertified materials in manufacturing and distribution systems
    - o observation of other relevant FSC rules, e.g. minimum requirements for FSC fiber content in assemblies.

Chain of Custody Requirements:

- Path taken by raw materials, processed materials and products from the forest to the consumer (end-user).
- Includes all successive stages of processing, transformation, manufacturing and distribution.
- **Forest:** Forest Management Certificate required
- **Transport:** COC is required if the transport to next stage involves change of ownership of material/product; not required if shippers or transport companies are handling goods owned by COC certified companies.
- **Supplier/Manufacturer:** COC is required for a wood products supplier and/or manufacturer that invoices FSC-certified wood products to a vendor.
- **Vendor:** COC is required for a vendor that invoices FSC-certified wood products to contractors and subcontractors; **all new wood on the project should identify which components are FSC-certified**.
- **End User:** COC is not required for contractors and subcontractors.

Vendors:

- Vendors are those companies that sell products to the project contractor or subcontractors.
- Collect all vendor invoices for permanently installed wood products, FSC-certified or not, purchased by the end users.
- Each vendor invoice must conform to the following requirements (**except as noted below**):
  o Identify all new wood products on a line item basis.
  o Identify FSC products on a line item basis [FSC Pure, FSC Mixed Credit, and FSC Mixed ([NN)%].
  o The dollar value of each line item must be shown.
  o The vendor's COC certificate number must be shown on any invoice that includes FSC products.
  o For FSC certified products, supply a letter stating the products are FSC Pure, FSC Mixed Credit, or FSC Mixed (NN)%
- **Exception:** If a line-item invoice would be dozens of pages long, the invoice may show an aggregate value of wood products; if the wood products are FSC certified, comply with the following requirements:
  o The vendor's COC number must be shown on the invoice.
  o The invoice must be supplemented by a letter from the vendor stating that the products invoiced are FSC certified.
  o The invoice or the letter must state whether the products are FSC Pure, FSC Mixed Credit, or FSC Mixed (NN)%.

Implementation:

- Establish a project goal for FSC-certified wood products and identify suppliers that can achieve this goal.
- During construction, ensure that the FSC-certified wood products are installed.
- Quantify the total percentage of FSC-certified wood products installed.

Calculations:

- List all the new wood on the project, both FSC certified and not, and identify which components are FSC-certified.
- Wood products that are not certified and "FSC Pure" and "FSC Mixed" are considered 100% FSC.
- Wood products identified as FSC Mixed (NN)% should be valued at the indicated percentage of their cost.
- **Wood products identified as FSC Recycled of FSC Recycled Credit do not qualify for this credit (use MR Cr4).**
- For assemblies, determine the amount of new wood as a % of total weight, volume or cost.
- For assemblies, determine the amount of FSC-certified wood as a % of total weight, volume or cost.
- The cost basis is useful for veneer.

Exemplary Performance: use 95% FSC certified wood content

Construction Submittal

Timeline/Team: Design Development – Owner, Architect or Design Team, Contractor; Design Phase – Architect should incorporate certified wood products; Construction – Contractor should review the project cost to verify that 50% of wood costs are FSC certified, obtain and retain COC certificates, and provide the documentation needed for the LEED certification application.

Regional Variations: Important in areas with poor forestry practices or high forest conversion rates.

O&M Considerations: Maintain information about the installed products for duplication, replacement and repair of certified products; encourage creation of a sustainable purchasing plan; provide operators with lists of installed products, their manufacturers and COC certificates (e.g. documentation used in the LEED application).

Indoor Environmental Quality (IEQ) NC 15 Pts, Schools 17-19 Pts, C&S 12 Pts

- Americans spend 90% of their time indoors.
- The EPA reports that indoor pollutant levels are 2 to 5 (and up to 100) times outdoors levels.
- The WHO reports that most of an individual's exposure to pollutants is from indoor air.
- 1987 and 1990 EPA reports designated indoor air pollution as a top environmental risk to public health.
- Health, liability and productivity drive IEQ improvements.

3 contaminants should be reduced to optimize tenants comfort and health:

1. Environmental Tobacco Smoke (ETS)
2. CO_2
3. Particulate Matter (lint, dirt, carpet fibers, dust mites, mold, bacteria, pollen, dander)

This credit category addresses the following:

1. Environmental concerns relating to IEQ
2. Occupants' health, safety and comfort
3. Energy consumption
4. Air change effectiveness
5. Air contaminant management

Important strategies:

1. Improve Ventilation
2. Manage Air Contaminants (ETS, CO_2, Particulates)
3. Specify Less Harmful Materials
4. Allow Occupants to Control Desired Settings
5. Provide Daylight and Views

Additional strategies for Schools and Core & Shell:

Schools: Influence background noise and acoustics in the following spaces,

Regularly Occupied – Classroom and Learning
Other Regularly Occupied
Not Regularly Occupied

Core & Shell: Influence the IEQ of common areas plus tenant build-out outside of C&S submittals.

IEQ Prerequisite 1 Minimum Indoor Air Quality Performance

Intent: Establish minimum indoor air quality (IAQ) performance to enhance indoor air quality in buildings, thus contributing to the comfort and well-being of the occupants.
Requirements:

CASE 1: Mechanically Ventilated Spaces
- Meet the minimum requirements of Sections 4 through 7 of ASHRAE 62.1-2007 (with errata, without addenda).
- Mechanical ventilation systems shall be designed using the **Ventilation Rate Procedure or the applicable local code, whichever is more stringent.**

Core & Shell (additional): Mechanical ventilation systems installed during C&S construction must be capable of meeting projected ventilation levels based on anticipated future tenant requirements.

CASE 2: Naturally Ventilated Spaces
- Naturally ventilated buildings shall comply with ASHRAE 62.1-2007, paragraph 5.1 (with errata, without addenda).

ASHRAE 62.1-2007 Considerations:

- Not for low-rise residential buildings (**use 62.2 for low-rise buildings**)
- New buildings, additions to existing buildings, and those changes to existing buildings identified in 62.1-2007
- **Chemical, physical and biological contaminants**
- **Occupant density, type of activity, floor area and type of ventilation system**
- Area related contaminants, e.g. off-gassing from building materials, furniture or other materials
- Make sure zone outside air (OA) requirements are met and system OA intake is adequate
- **"Zone" OA flow** should reflect **"zone air distribution effectiveness" (E_z). "MZ" (multizone) OA flow** should reflect **system ventilation efficiency of the air distribution configuration" (E_v).**
- For natural ventilation, the **space must be permanently open to and within 25 feet of operable wall or roof openings** with the opening's **operable ft^2/occupiable $ft^2 \geq 4\%$.** Interior spaces without direct openings to the outdoors can be ventilated through adjoining rooms if the openings between rooms are unobstructed and at least **8% or 25 ft^2 of the area** is free.
- For mixed-mode ventilation, meet 62.1-2007 regardless of the mode; use an acceptable engineering calculation methodology.

<u>Implementation:</u>
- **For mechanical ventilation systems use MERV6 filters or better, as rated according to ASHRAE 52.2.**
- Design ventilation systems to meet or exceed the minimum outdoor air ventilation rates described in 62.1-2007.
- Balance the impacts of ventilation rates on energy use and IAQ to optimize for energy efficiency and occupant comfort.
- Use ASHRAE 62.1-2007 Users Manual (w errata, w/o addenda) for detailed guidance on meeting referenced requirements.
- Active Ventilation = Mechanical; Passive Ventilation = Natural; Mixed-mode Ventilation = both
- Approved ASHRAE addenda may be used for this prerequisite, but must be applied consistently across all credits.

<u>Calculations:</u>
- Breathing Zone OA flowrate = V_{bz} = CFM/P x P + CFM/ft^2 x ft^2 (from Table 6-1, 62.1-2007), where P = number of people.
- Zone OA flowrate = V_{bz} / E_z (E_z from Table 6-2, 62.1-2007).
- Use the methodology of the Ventilation Rate Procedure given in Section 6.2 of ASHRAE 62.1-2007.
- Table 6.1 in Section 62.1 lists Minimum Ventilation Rates in Breathing Zones according to use, occupancy, and floor area.

Exemplary Performance: na
Design Submittal

Timeline/Team: Design Phase – Architect, Mechanical Engineer, Owner, Tenants, Facility Managers, Maintenance Personnel
Regional Variations: na

O&M Considerations: For mechanical ventilation, provide rate procedure data to operators for updating with actual occupancy; provide maintenance personnel with information needed to understand, maintain and adjust ventilation systems; establish procedures to test and maintain exhaust systems.

IEQ Prerequisite 2 Environmental Tobacco Smoke (ETS) Control

Intent: Prevent (Schools) or **minimize (NC and C&S)** exposure of building occupants, indoor surfaces and ventilation air distribution systems to Environmental Tobacco Smoke (ETS).

Requirements:

<u>**NEW CONSTRUCTION AND CORE & SHELL ONLY**</u>

CASE 1: All Projects

OPTION 1
- Prohibit smoking in the building.
- Prohibit on-property smoking <u>within 25 ft from entries, OA intakes and operable windows</u>.
- Provide <u>signage</u> to <u>allow</u> smoking <u>in designated</u> areas, <u>prohibit in designated</u> areas, <u>or prohibit on entire property</u>.

OPTION 2
- Prohibit smoking in the building <u>except in designated smoking areas</u>.
- Prohibit on-property smoking <u>within 25 ft from entries, OA intakes and operable windows</u>.
- Provide <u>signage</u> to <u>allow</u> smoking <u>in designated</u> areas, <u>prohibit in designated</u> areas, <u>or prohibit on entire property</u>.
- Locate designated smoking rooms to effectively contain, capture and remove ETS from the building.
- At a minimum, the smoking room must have an "isolation" room and an "Ante" room (foyer with exhaust air only), and:
    - be directly exhausted to the outdoors
    - be located away from air intakes and building entry paths
    - have no recirculation of ETS-containing air to the non-smoking area of the building
    - be enclosed with impermeable deck-to-deck partitions
- With the doors to the smoking room closed, operate the exhaust to create a negative pressure differential at an average of 0.02" water gauge and a minimum of 0.004" water guage.
- Verify smoking room differential pressure via 15 minute tests (minimum one measurement every 10 seconds) of the differential pressure (1) in the smoking room with respect to each adjacent area, and (2) in each adjacent vertical chase with the doors to the smoking room closed.
- The testing will be conducted with each space configured for worst case conditions of transport of air from the smoking rooms to adjacent spaces with the smoking rooms' doors closed to the adjacent spaces.

CASE 2: Residential and Hospitality Projects Only

- Prohibit smoking in the building <u>except in designated smoking areas</u>.
- Locate any <u>exterior designated</u> smoking areas, including balconies where smoking is permitted, <u>at least 25 ft from entries, OA intakes and operable windows opening to common areas</u>.
- <u>Prohibit</u> on-property smoking <u>within 25 ft from entries, OA intakes and operable windows</u>.
- Provide <u>signage</u> to <u>allow</u> smoking <u>in designated</u> areas, <u>prohibit in designated</u> areas, or <u>prohibit on entire property</u>.
- Minimize uncontrolled pathways for ETS transfer between individual residential units by sealing walls, ceilings, floors, chases.
- Weather-strip doors from residential units to common hallways and doors/windows from units to the exterior.
- Demonstrate acceptable sealing of residential units by a **blower door test**.
- Residential units must demonstrate < 1.25 in^2 leakage area per 100 ft^2 enclosed area.

<u>**SCHOOLS ONLY:**</u>

- Same as Case 1, Option 1

Calculations: na
Exemplary Performance: na
Design Submittal:

Timeline/Team: Building/site smoking policy is drafted by facility manager and signed by facility manager, property manager, or owner; enforcement is by facility manager and grounds keeper over the life of the building.
Regional Variations: Varies state to state.
O&M Considerations: Communicate ETS control plan to occupants, establish plan for reinforcement, designate implementer.

IEQ Prerequisite 3 Minimum Acoustical Performance (Schools Only)

Intent (for Schools only): Provide classrooms that are quiet so that teachers can speak to the class without straining their voices and students can effectively communicate with each other and the teacher.

Requirements:
- Design classrooms and other core learning spaces to include sufficient sound-absorptive finishes for compliance with **reverberation time (RT) requirements as specified in ANSI Standard S12.60-2002**, Acoustical Performance Criteria, design Requirements and Guidelines for Schools.
- **Achieve ≤ 45 dBA background noise level from HVAC systems** in classrooms and other core learning spaces.

<u>AND</u>

CASE 1: Classrooms and Core Learning Spaces < 20,000 ft^3

OPTION 1
- Confirm that **100% of all ceiling areas** (excluding lights, diffusers and grilles) in all classrooms and core learning spaces are finished with a material that has a Noise Reduction Coefficient **(NRC) of 0.70 or higher**.

OPTION 2
- Confirm that the **total area of acoustical** wall panels, ceiling finishes and other sound-absorbent finishes **equals or exceeds the total ceiling area** of the room (excluding lights, diffusers and grilles). Materials must have an **NRC of 0.70 or higher** to be included in the calculation.

CASE 2: Classrooms and Core Learning Spaces ≥ 20,000 ft^3

- Confirm through calculations from S12.60-2002 that all classrooms and core learning spaces ≥ 20,000 ft^3 are design to have an **RT ≤ 1.5 seconds**.

- **Background noise and reverberation** affect children, whose ability to distinguish sounds is not fully developed.
- Students are more likely to become distracted, have difficulty retaining information, and have trouble engaging in learning.
- Children with temporary hearing loss (15%), speech impairments and learning disabilities are especially affected.
- Planning for an effective acoustic environment improves teacher effectiveness, student performance and educational quality.
- Poor acoustics cause teachers' vocal fatigue and absenteeism, and students' remedial instruction and grade repetition.

ANSI/ASHRAE S12.60-2002: acoustical performance criteria &design requirements for classrooms & other learning spaces.
ASHRAE Handbook, Chapter 47 Sound and Vibration Control, 2007 HVAC App's: acceptable sound and vibration levels.

<u>Background Noise</u>
- Background noise is **measured in dBA**, the A-weighted decibel sound pressure level measured on a non-linear scale.
- An **increase of 10 dBA doubles the loudness**, e.g. 90 dBA (jackhammer) is twice as loud as 80 dBA.(busy cafeteria).
- S12.60-2002 describes effective methods and strategies for HVAC noise control and for RT calculation and design.
- ASHRAE Chapter 47, 2007 HVAC Applications provides detailed methods for reducing noise transmission from HVAC sys.
- For noise control, Annex B of S12.60-2002; for best practices and calculation methods, ASHRAE Ch. 47, 2007 HVAC App's.
    - Option 1: ceiling finish materials with an NRC ≥ 0.70 for 100% of the ceiling (excl. diffusers, grilles, light fixtures).
    - Option 2: ceiling and wall finish materials with an NRC ≥ 0.70, and the total acoustical ceiling and wall area is ≥ 100% of the ceiling area (excluding diffusers, grilles, light fixtures).

- **HVAC equipment is typically the primary source of noise in classrooms**.
- Suggested ways to reduce background noise:
    - Add storm windows.
    - Replace existing windows with thermal insulating windows (select with high STC rating).
    - Install specially fabricated sound-reducing windows.
    - Check doors for gaps larger than 1/16 inch.
    - Add good quality crop seals and gaskets.
    - Install tight fitting solid core doors with seals and gaskets.
    - Install special sound control doors if adjacent spaces are very noisy

IEQ Prerequisite 3 (cont.)

Reverberation Time
- RT is the time it takes for the **level of a steady sound to decay by 60 dB after the sound has stopped**.
- RT has the most effect on speech intelligibility in the **500, 1000 and 2000** Hz frequency bands.
- S12.60-2002 requires calculation of RT at each of these 3 frequencies.
- The **noise reduction coefficient (NRC)** is a single number rating for the **sound-absorptive properties of a material**.
- The NRC is the arithmetic average of sound absorption coefficients for a material at **250, 500, 1000 and 2000** HZ.
- RT must be calculated for 500, 1000 and 2000 HZ; each RT must meet the S1260-2002 requirement. Ex. for 500 Hz:

  V = volume of room in ft^3
  A = total sound absorption in the room for a given frequency
  A_{500} = **$sum(a_n s_n)$**, where a_n is the sound absorption coefficient of material n and s_n is the total surface area for material n.

  $RT_{500} = 0.049 \times V/A_{500}$

- Hard surfaces in a room raise the RT, reduce speech intelligibility and increase overall loudness.
- **RT must not exceed 1.5 seconds at 500, 1000 and 2000 Hz in rooms 20,000 ft^3 or larger**.
- Suggested ways to reduce reverberation:
    o Replace existing low-NRC acoustical ceiling tiles with high-NRC acoustical tiles.
    o Add new suspended acoustical tile (if height permits), or attach acoustical tile to the existing ceiling.
    o Add sound-absorbing panels high on the walls at the sides and rear of room.
    o If the classroom has a very high ceiling (over 11'), add acoustical panels on both ceiling and walls.
- **Carpet adds little to reverberation control** but is useful for controlling self-noise, e.g. chair movement by young children.

Sound Transmission
- Specific sound transmission performance is not required for compliance with this prerequisite (**See IEQ Credit 9**).

Ways to Reduce HVAC Noise
- Add custom built sound enclosure around each unit.
- Add sound lined ductwork to the unit to attenuate air distribution.
- Use quieter split systems or through-the-wall models.
- Increase the open area at grilles and diffusers.
- Rebalance the system to reduce air volume delivered to the classroom.
- Relocate ductwork and diffusers away from teaching locations.
- Add duct length to attenuate noise.
- Add sound lining to ducts.

Additional Ways to Reduce Room Noise
- Rearrange seating; put tennis balls or rubber tips on chair legs; avoid open classrooms; diminish the sound from computer keyboards; locate all large pieces of computer equipment in a separate room.

Implementation:
- Select quieter HVAC systems and locate HVAC units centrally.
- Simple supply air ducting, and to a lesser extent return air ducting, will help meet background noise criteria.
- Use acoustic liner in ductwork to minimize sound transmission.
- Use absorptive materials and treatments to decrease RT.
- Annex C, Section 3 of S12.60-2002 provides guidelines for controlling reverberation in classrooms.

Calculations: see above for Background Noise and Reverberation Time
Exemplary Performance: na
Design Submittal

Timeline/Team: Design Phase – Mechanical Engineer, Electrical Engineer and Contractor consider acoustics; involve an acoustical consultant; involve teachers and staff.
Regional Variations: Regional factors influence ambient noise around schools, e.g. wind in the Midwest or fog on the coast.
O&M Considerations: Establish a policy for continued use of acoustical best practices during building operation; help operators find appropriate products and materials for repairs or alterations by providing them with a list of compliant products.

IEQ Credit 1 Outdoor Air Delivery Monitoring (1, 1, 1)

Intent: Provide capacity for ventilation system monitoring to help sustain occupant comfort and well-being.

Requirements:

- Install permanent monitoring systems that provide feedback on ventilation system performance to ensure that ventilation systems maintain design minimum ventilation requirements.
- Configure all monitoring equipment to generate an <u>alarm</u> when <u>CFM or CO_2</u> level <u>varies by 10%</u> or more <u>from the design value</u>, either via a <u>BAS alarm to the building operator</u> <u>or</u> via an <u>audio/visual alert to the building occupants</u>.

CASE 1: MECHANICALLY VENTILATED SPACES:

- Monitor CO_2 in all **densely** occupied spaces ($\geq$ **25 people per 1000 ft^2**) at **3' to 6' above the floor**.
- Provide a direct **OA cfm measurement** device capable **of** measuring **minimum intake OA cfm accurate to $\pm$ 15%** of **design minimum** intake **OA cfm** (per 62.1-2007 with errata, without addenda) for mechanical ventilation systems **where $\geq$ 20%** of the **design SA cfm serves non-densely** occupied spaces.

CASE 2: NATURALLY VENTILATED SPACES:

- Monitor CO_2 within all naturally ventilated spaces at **3' to 6' above the floor**.
- <u>One</u> CO_2 sensor may be used <u>to represent multiple non-densely</u> occupied spaces <u>if</u> the design <u>uses passive stack(s) or other means to induce airflow</u> through the spaces <u>equally and simultaneously without intervention by occupants</u>.

<u>**Instrumentation:**</u>
- Pitot Tubes, Venturi Meters, Vane Anemometers
- Detect when OA cfm is **15% below design**

<u>**Demand Controlled Ventilation (DCV):**</u>
- OA cfm fluctuates based on CO_2 monitor readings (**alert usually at <u>1000 ppm</u>**).
- <u>Normal</u> CO_2 concentration detected may vary from <u>300 to 500 ppm</u> based on location, time of day and neighbors.

Breathing Zone: <u>3' to 6' above the floor, 2' from walls or fixed AC equipment</u>

Implementation:

- Install CO_2 and airflow measurement equipment and feed the information to the HVAC system and/or BAS for action.
- If such automatic controls aren't feasible with the building systems, use the measurement equipment to trigger alarms that inform building operators or occupants of a possible deficiency in outdoor air delivery.
- For HVAC systems with limited airflow monitoring capabilities, use differential CO_2 monitoring between outside and space air and a means for AHUs to provide more OA **if the differential exceeds 530 ppm. (OA is usually 400 ppm)**.
- <u>Approved ASHRAE addenda may be used for this credit, but must be applied consistently across all credits</u>

Calculations: na

Exemplary Performance: na

Design Submittal

Timeline/Team: Design team specifies placement of OA sensors, specifically the Mechanical Engineer.

Regional Variations: Consider time of day fluctuations near highways; consider combustion or other contaminant sources.

O&M Considerations: Educate the facility manager; establish appropriate setpoints and control sequences, and procedures and schedules for inspection, calibration, testing and maintenance of monitoring equipment. Use sensors that require calibration every five years at a minimum.

IEQ Credit 2 Increased Ventilation (1, 1, 1)

Intent: Provide additional outdoor air ventilation to improve indoor air quality for improved occupant comfort, well-being and productivity.

Requirements:

CASE 1: MECHANICALLY VENTILATED SPACES:

- Increase breathing zone OA cfm to all occupied spaces by at least **30% above the minimum** requirements of 62.1-2007 (with errata, without addenda) as **determined by IEQ Prerequisite 1**.

CASE 2: NATURALLY VENTILATED SPACES:

- Meet recommendations set forth in the **Carbon Trust Good Practice <u>Guide 237</u>** (1998).
- Determine that **natural ventilation** is an **effective** strategy by **following** the <u>**flow diagram**</u> process in **Figure 1.18** of the Chartered Institution of Building Services Engineers **(CIBSE) Applications Manual 10: 2005, Natural Ventilation in Non-domestic Buildings, <u>AND</u>**

<u>OPTION 1:</u>
Use diagrams and calculations to **show** that the **design meets** recommendations set forth in the **CIBSE Applications Manual 10: 2005**, Natural Ventilation in Non-domestic Buildings,

<u>OPTION 2:</u>
Use a **macroscopic, multi-zone, Analytic Model** to **predict** that **room-by-room airflows** will **effectively** naturally **ventilate per 62.1-2007** Chapter 6 (w errata, w/o addenda) **for at least 90% of the occupied spaces**.

Implementation:

- <u>Mechanically</u> Ventilated Spaces: Use heat recovery to minimize additional energy consumption associated with higher rates.
- <u>Naturally</u> Ventilates Spaces: Follow the 8 steps in the "<u>Guide</u>" (1) Develop design requirements (2) Plan airflow paths (3) Identify building uses and features needing special attention (4) Determine ventilation requirements (5) Estimate external driving pressures (6) Select types of ventilation devices (7) Size ventilation devices (8) Analyze the design.
- Use public domain software, e.g. CONTAM and LoopDA, to analytically predict room-by-room airflows.
- <u>Approved ASHRAE addenda may be used for this credit, but must be applied consistently across all credits.</u>

Calculations:

- **Mechanical:** Build table and spreadsheet with **Ventilation Rate Procedure calculations to show 30% above** 62.1-2007 guidelines (the **same calculation may be used to document both IEQ Prerequisite 1 and IEQ Credit 2**).
- **Natural:** Provide sample calculations to demonstrate **compliance with CIBSE AM 10** <u>and</u> Carbon Trust Good Practice **Guide 237**, <u>or</u> **provide** the **room-by-room OA cfm predicted by an Analytical Model** and a comparison to the minimum requirements of 62.1-2007 Chapter 6.

Exemplary Performance: na

Design Submittal

Timeline/Team: Consider building size and type, climate, economics and organization, site conditions, and design.

Regional Variations: More practical for mild climates, as are natural ventilation and passive air conditioning.

O&M Considerations: For mechanical ventilation, provide rate procedure data to operators for updating with actual occupancy; provide maintenance personnel with information needed to understand, maintain and adjust ventilation systems; establish procedures to test and maintain exhaust systems.

IEQ Credit 3/3.1 Construction IAQ Management Plan - During Construction (1, 1, 1)

<u>**Note: (This Credit is called IEQ Credit 3 for Core & Shell because there is no IEQ Credit 3.2 for Core & Shell)**</u>

Intent: Reduce indoor air quality problems resulting from the construction or renovation process in order to help sustain the comfort and well-being of construction workers and building occupants.

Requirements: Develop and implement an IAQ Management Plan for the construction and pre-occupancy phases of the building as follows:

- During construction meet or exceed the recommended **Control Measures of the SMACNA IAQ Guidelines** for Occupied Buildings Under Construction, 2nd Edition 2007, ANSI/SMACNA 008-2008 (Chapter 3).
- Protect stored on-site or installed absorptive materials from moisture damage, e.g. carpet.
- **If permanently installed AHUs are used during construction,** MERV 8 filtration media shall be used **at each return air grille** as per 52.2-1999 (w errata, w/o addenda), **AND replace all filtration media immediately prior to occupancy.**

<u>**Schools (additional):**</u>

- Prohibit smoking inside the building and within 25' of building entrances once the building is enclosed.

Considerations:

- <u>Coordinate with IEQ Credits 3.2 and 5</u> to determine the appropriate specifications and schedules for filtration media.

- If possible, <u>avoid using permanently installed AHUs</u> for temporary heating or cooling during construction.

- <u>Control Measures of the SMACNA IAQ Guidelines for ….</u>: (1) HVAC Protection (2) Source Control (3) Pathway Interruption (4) Housekeeping (5) Scheduling

- The General Contractor must provide data and documentation.

Implementation:

- Adopt an IAQ management plan to protect the HVAC system during construction; control pollutant sources and interrupt contamination pathways.
- Sequence the installation of materials to avoid contamination of absorptive materials such as insulation, carpeting, ceiling tile and gypsum wallboard.
- Coordinate with IEQ Cr 3.2 and Cr 5 to determine the appropriate specifications and schedules for filtration media.
- If possible, avoid using permanently installed AHUs for temporary heating/cooling during construction.
- Consult the LEED 2009 Reference Guide for more detailed information on how to ensure the well-being of construction workers and building occupants if permanently installed AHU's must be used during construction.
- <u>Approved ASHRAE addenda may be used for this credit, but must be applied consistently across all credits</u>

Calculations: na

Exemplary Performance: <u>**Core & Shell only**</u> – Projects that <u>require/enforce</u> a construction IAQ plan <u>for 100% of tenant spaces</u>.

Construction Submittal

Timeline/Team: Consider demolition, construction and finish materials; install products that emit VOCs before installing absorbent materials; give plan to subs and field personnel; post a copy of the plan and maintain a photo log.

Regional Variations: na

O&M Considerations: Provide the facility manager with a copy of the plan to facilitate using the same plan for future alterations and additions.

IEQ Credit 3.2 Construction IAQ Management Plan - Before Occupancy (1, 1, 0)

Intent (for NC and Schools only): Reduce indoor air quality problems resulting from the construction or renovation process in order to help sustain the comfort and well-being of construction workers and building occupants.

Requirements:

Develop an IAQ Management Plan and implement the plan **after installation of all finishes, completion of building cleaning, and before occupancy**:

OPTION 1 - Flush-out (Note: All finishes must be installed prior to flush-out)

PATH 1
- After construction and **prior to occupancy** and with all interior finishes installed, flush-out with a total of **14,000 ft^3 OA per ft^2 floor area** while **maintain**ing an internal **T $\geq$ 60 deg** and **RH $\leq$ 60%.**

PATH 2
- **If occupancy is desired** prior to completion of the flush-out, the space may be occupied following delivery of **3,500 ft^3 OA per ft^2 floor area**.
- Once the space is occupied, **maintain minimum OA at 0.30 cfm/ ft^2**, **OR** at the **rate determined in IEQ Prerequisite 1, whichever is greater**.
- During each day of the flush-out, ventilation shall **begin a minimum of 3 hours prior to occupancy and continue during occupancy**.
- These conditions shall be maintained **until** a total of **14,000 ft^3 OA per ft^2 floor area** has been delivered to the space.

OPTION 2 - Air Quality Testing
- Conduct a baseline IAQ test after construction ends and prior to occupancy using testing protocols consistent with the **US EPA Compendium of Methods for the Determination of Air Pollutants in Indoor Air** and as additionally detailed in the LEED Reference Guide.
- Demonstrate that the contaminant **maximum concentrations** listed in the Reference Guide for **Formaldehyde** (27 ppb), **Particulates** (50 micrograms/m^3), **TVOCs** (500 micrograms/m^3), **4-PCH** (6.5 micrograms/m^3 and only required if carpets and fabrics with SBR latex backing material are installed as part of the base building systems), and **CO** (9ppm and no greater than 2 ppm above outdoor levels) **are not exceeded**.
- Repeat the flush-out until the requirements are achieved, taking samples from the same locations as in the first test.
- Sample the air as follows:
  - Prior to occupancy: during normal occupancy hours, at normal start times and at minimum design OA.
  - After all interior finishes are installed [non-fixed furnishings encouraged but not required to be installed].
  - For each system, one per 25,000 sq.ft. or one for each contiguous floor area, whichever area is bigger.
  - Between 3' and 6' from the floor and over a 4-hour period.

Implementation:

- **Prior to occupancy, perform a building flush-out or test the air contaminant levels** in the building.
- The flush-out is often used where occupancy is not required immediately upon substantial completion of construction.
- IAQ testing can minimize schedule impacts but may be more costly.
- Coordinate with IEQ Cr 3.1 and Cr 5 to determine the appropriate specs and schedules for filtration media.
- **Finishes used in tenant build-outs must be addressed in order to qualify for this credit**.
- Approved ASHRAE addenda may be used for this credit, but must be applied consistently across all credits

Calculations: Na
Exemplary Performance: na
Construction Submittal

Timeline/Team: Design Phase – include language requiring the GC to develop and implement a plan; Post Construction – after construction and installation of all finishes (including furniture and furnishing), implement the plan.

Regional Variations: Maintain indoor air temperature $\geq$ 60° and RH $\leq$ 60% (consider seasonal variations and project schedule).
O&M Considerations: Provide the facility manager with a copy of the plan to facilitate using the same plan for future alterations and additions.

IEQ Credit 4.1 Low-Emitting Materials - Adhesives & Sealants (1, 1, 1*)

*Schools choose 4 credits from IEQ Credit 4.1 through IEQ Credit 4.6.

Intent: Reduce the quantity of indoor air contaminants that are odorous, irritating and/or harmful to the comfort and well-being of installers and occupants.

Requirements:

New Construction and C&S:

All adhesives, sealants and sealant primers used **on the interior** of the building (defined as **inside the weatherproofing** and **applied on-site**) shall comply with the requirements and **limits** in the following reference standards:

- **Adhesives, Sealants and Sealant Primers:**

  South Coast Air Quality Management District (**SCAQMD**) Rule #1168. See table below for **VOC limits (7/1/2005)**:

Architectural Applications	VOC Limit [g/L less water]	Specialty Applications	VOC Limit [g/L less water]
Indoor Capet Adhesives	50	PVC Welding	510
Carpet Pad Adhesives	50	CPVC Welding	490
Wood Flooring Adhesives	100	ABS Welding	325
Rubber Floor Adhesives	60	Plastic Cement Welding	250
Subfloor Adhesives	50	Adhesive Primer for Plastic	550
Ceramic Tile Adhesives	65	Contact Adhesive	80
VCT & Asphalt Adhesives	50	Special Purpose Contact Adhesive	250
Drywall & Panel Adhesives	50	Structural Wood Member Adhesive	140
Cove Base Adhesives	50	Sheet Applied Rubber Lining Operations	850
Multipurpose Constr Adhesives	70	Top & Trim Adhesive	250
Structural Glazing Adhesives	100		
Substrate Specific Applications		**Sealants**	
Metal to Metal	30	Architectural	250
Plastic Foams	50	Non-membrane Roof	300
Porous Material (except wood)	50	Roadway	250
Wood	30	Single-ply Roof Membrane	450
Fiberglass	80	Other	420
Sealant Primers			
Architectural Non-porous	250		
Architectural Porous	775		
Other	750		

- **Aerosol Adhesives:**

  Green Seal Standard for Commercial Adhesives GS-36 requirements in effect on October 19, 2000:

Aerosol Adhesives	VOC Weight [g/L minus water]
General purpose mist spray	65% VOCs by weight
General purpose web spray	55% VOCs by weight
Special purpose aerosol adhesives (all types)	70% VOCs by weight

Schools:

All adhesives, sealants and sealant primers used **on the interior** of the building (defined as **inside the weatherproofing** and **applied on-site**) must meet the testing and product requirements of the **California** Department of Health Services Standard Practice for the **Testing of Volatile Organic Emissions** from Various Sources Using Small-Scale Environmental Chambers, incl. 2004 Addenda. **This standard sets a limit on the rate that off-gassing may occur.**

IEQ Credit 4.1 (cont.)

Indoor Adhesive Sealant and/or Sealant Primer: <u>applied on-site</u>, <u>inside of the building's weatherproofing system</u>
Non-porous Sealant: for plastic, metal and other materials that don't have openings that absorb or discharge fluids
Porous Sealant: for wood, fabric, paper, corrugated paperboard and plastic foam
Sealant: substance with adhesive properties used to fill, seal or waterproof gaps or joints (sealant primers and caulks)
Primer: applied to a substrate to improve adhesion of subsequently applied adhesive
VOCs: volatile organic compounds that participate in atmospheric photochemical reactions; gases at room temperature
Not VOCs: CO, CO2, Carbonic Acid, metallic carbides and carbonates, ammonium carbonate

Implementation:

- Specify low-VOC materials in construction documents.
- Ensure that VOC limits are clearly stated in each section of the specs where adhesives and sealants are addressed.
- Common products to evaluate:
    - General construction adhesives
    - Flooring adhesives
    - Fire-stopping sealants
    - Caulking
    - Duct sealants
    - Plumbing adhesives
    - Cove base adhesives
- Review product cut sheets, MSD sheets, signed attestations or other official literature from the manufacturer.
- In the manufacturer's literature, clearly identify the VOC contents or compliance with reference standards

<u>**Schools:**</u>
- Acoustical elements within the building may require special installation considerations.
- The Collaborative for High Performance Schools (CHPS) Best Practices Manual, 206, Low-Emitting Materials (LEM) Table contains guidelines and strategies for effective acoustical performance in school buildings. Products listed are certified by the manufacturer and an independent laboratory to meet the CHPS LEM criteria.

Calculations: Determining a VOC budget is one way to achieve compliance. Consider paints and adhesives separately. Compare baseline to the design case.

Exemplary Performance: na

Construction Submittal: General Contractor must provide data and documentation

Timeline/Team: Requirements for IEQ Credit 4 (Low-Emitting Materials) should be noted in the project Specifications; clearly state credit requirements in the Specs.

Regional Variations: na

O&M Considerations: na

IEQ Credit 4.2 Low-Emitting Materials - Paints & Coatings (1, 1, 1*)

*Schools choose 4 credits from IEQ Credit 4.1 through IEQ Credit 4.6.

Intent: Reduce the quantity of indoor air contaminants that are odorous, irritating and/or harmful to the comfort and well-being of installers and occupants.

Requirements:

New Construction and C&S:

Paints and coatings used <u>on the interior</u> of the building (defined as <u>inside the weatherproofing</u> and <u>applied on-site</u>) shall comply with the requirements and **limits** in the following reference standards:

- **Architectural paints, coatings and primers applied to interior walls and ceilings:**

  Do not exceed the VOC content limits in **Green Seal Standard GS-11, Paints**, 1st Edition, May20, 1993

- **Anti-corrosive and anti-rust paints applied to interior ferrous metal substrates:**

  Do not exceed the VOC content limits in **Green Seal Standard GS-03, Anti-Corrosive Paints**, 2nd Ed, January 7, 1997

- **Clear wood finishes, floor coatings, stains, sealers and shellacs applied to interior elements:**

  Do not exceed the VOC content limits in **SCAQMD Rule 1113, Architectural Coatings**, January 1, 2004

Schools:
All paints and coatings installed in the building **interior** must meet the testing and product requirements of the CA Dept. of Health Services Standard Practice for the Testing of Volatile Organic Emissions from Various Sources Using Small-Scale Environmental Chambers, incl. 2004 Addenda.

Note: Use of VOC budgets is an alternative compliance path that allows for specialty applications for which there is no low VOC product option.

Paint: liquid, liquefiable or mastic composition that is converted to a solid adherent film after application
Anti-corrosive Paints: formulated and recommended for use in preventing the corrosion of ferrous metal substrates
Flat: gloss of < 15 on an 85 degree meter or < 5 on a 60 degree meter
Non-flat: gloss of ≥ 15 on an 85 degree meter of ≥ 5 on a 60 degree meter

Implementation:

- Specify low-VOC paints and coatings in construction documents.
- Ensure that VOC limits are clearly stated in each section of the specs where paints and coatings are addressed.
- Track the VOC content of all interior paints and coatings during construction.

Schools:
- Acoustical elements within the building may require special installation considerations.
- The Collaborative for High Performance Schools (CHPS) Best Practices Manual, 206, Low-Emitting Materials (LEM) Table contains guidelines and strategies for effective acoustical performance in school buildings. Products listed are certified by the manufacturer and an independent laboratory to meet the CHPS LEM criteria.

Calculations: Na
Exemplary Performance: na
Construction Submittal

Timeline/Team: Requirements for IEQ Credit 4 (Low-Emitting Materials) should be noted in the project Specifications; clearly state credit requirements in the Specs.
Regional Variations: na
O&M Considerations: (1) Establish a sustainable purchasing policy (2) Provide operators with a list of compliant products (3) Provide maintenance personnel with information to aid color matching to original products (4) Use fewer types of paints and coatings.

IEQ Credit 4.3 Low-Emitting Materials - Flooring Systems (1, 1, 1*)

*Schools choose 4 credits from IEQ Credit 4.1 through IEQ Credit 4.6.

Intent: Reduce the quantity of indoor air contaminants that are odorous, irritating and/or harmful to the comfort and well-being of installers and occupants.

Requirements for flooring systems:

New Construction and C&S:
OPTION 1

- All **carpet** installed in the building interior shall meet the testing and product requirements of the:
  Carpet and Rug Institute's Green Label program (CRI is a trade organization).
- All carpet adhesive shall meet the requirements of IEQ Cr 4.1: VOC limit of 50 g/L.
- All **hard surface flooring** must be certified by an independent third-party as compliant with the:
  FloorScore standard (as of the date of this Rating System, or more stringent version)
- Flooring products covered by **FloorScore** include:
  Vinyl, linoleum, laminate flooring, wood flooring, ceramic flooring, rubber flooring, wall base, associated sundries.
- An alternative compliance path using FloorScore is acceptable for achieving this credit as follows:
  100% of non-carpet finished flooring must be FloorScore-certified and must be at least 25% of the finished floor area.
- **Concrete, wood, bamboo and cork floor finishes** must meet the SCAQMD requirements of IEQ Cr 4.2 for clear wood finishes, floor coatings, stains, sealers and shellacs applied to interior elements.
- **Tile setting adhesives and grout** must meet SCAQMD Rule 1168. VOC limits correspond to an effective date of July 1, 2005 and rule amendment date of January 7, 2005.

New Construction, Shools and C&S:
OPTION 2

- All flooring systems must meet the testing and product requirements of the California Department of Health Services Standard Practice for The Testing of Volatile Organic Emissions from Various Sources using Small-Scale Environmental Chambers, including 2004 Addenda.

Note: FloorScore is a voluntary, independent certification program that tests and certifies hard surface flooring and associated products for compliance with criteria adopted in California for VOC emissions, aka Section 1350. As part of certification, a 3rd party certifier, Scientific Certification Systems (SCS): (1) works with manufacturers to ID appropriate samples for testing (2) reviews VOC emission test reports from independent labs for individual products (3) determines if test results meet CA Section 1350 requirements (4) inspects plants in order to define the permitted use of the FloorScore seal.

Implementation:
- Clearly specify the requirements for product testing and/or certification in the construction documents.
- Select products that are certified under the Green Label Plus program or tested by qualified independent labs
- Green Label Plus program for carpets tests VOC emission in **micrograms/meter/hour** per CRI and Calif. rules

Schools:
- Acoustical elements within the building may require special installation considerations.
- The Collaborative for High Performance Schools (CHPS) Best Practices Manual, 206, Low-Emitting Materials (LEM) Table contains guidelines and strategies for effective acoustical performance in school buildings. Products listed are certified by the manufacturer and an independent laboratory to meet the CHPS LEM criteria.

Calculations: Na
Exemplary Performance: na
Construction Submittal
Timeline/Team: Requirements for IEQ Credit 4 (Low-Emitting Materials) should be noted in the project Specifications; clearly state credit requirements in the Specs.
Regional Variations: na
O&M Considerations: (1) Establish a sustainable purchasing policy (2) Provide operators with a list of compliant products. Use carpet tiles for easier repair. Use fewer flooring products. Give operators information about specialty flooring materials maint.

IEQ Credit 4.4 Low-Emitting Materials - Composite Wood & Agrifiber Products (1, 1, 1*)

*Schools choose 4 credits from IEQ Credit 4.1 through IEQ Credit 4.6.

Intent: Reduce the quantity of indoor air contaminants that are odorous, irritating and/or harmful to the comfort and well-being of installers and occupants.

Requirements:

<u>New Construction and C&S:</u>
- Composite wood and agrifiber products used on the interior of the building (defined as <u>inside the weatherproofing</u> and <u>applied on-site</u>) shall contain **no added urea-formaldehyde resins**.
- Laminating adhesives used to fabricate on-site and shop-applied composite wood and agrifiber assemblies shall contain **no added urea-formaldehyde resins**.
- Composite wood and agrifiber products are defined as follows:
    - Particleboard
    - Medium Density Fiberboard (MDF)
    - Plywood
    - Wheatboard
    - Strawboard
    - Panel Substrates
    - Door Cores
- **Materials considered fixtures, furniture and equipment (FF&E) are not base building elements and are not included**.

<u>Schools:</u>
- All composite wood and agrifiber products installed in the building must meet the testing and product requirements of the <u>California</u> Department of Health Services Standard Practice for The Testing of Volatile Organic Emissions from Various Sources <u>using Small-Scale Environmental Chambers</u>, including 2004 Addenda.

Agrifiber Board: composite panel made from <u>agricultural waste</u> fibers <u>mixed with</u> <u>resins</u> (cereal, sugarcane, sunflower husks, walnut shells, coconut husks.

Composite Wood: wood or plant <u>particles or fibers</u> <u>bonded together by</u> a <u>synthetic resin or binder</u> (plywood, particle-board, OSB, MDF, composite door cores.

Fomaldehyde: naturally occurring VOC; carcinogenic; problems when concentration in the air is above <u>0.1 PPM</u>.

Urea-formaldehyde: combination of urea and formaldehyde used in some glues; <u>may emit formaldehyde at room temp</u>.

Phenol-formaldehyde: used for exterior products, many of which are used inside; <u>off-gases only at high temperature</u>.

The following conditions describe which products must comply with the requirements:
- Product is <u>inside</u> of the building's <u>waterproofing</u> system.
- Composite <u>components</u> used <u>in assemblies</u> must be included, <u>e.g. door cores</u>, panel substrates, etc.
- Product is <u>part of the base building</u> systems.

Implementation:
- Specify wood and agrifiber products that contain no added urea-formaldehyde resins.
- Specify laminating adhesives for field and shop applied assemblies that contain no added urea-formaldehyde resins.
- Review product cut sheets, MSD sheets, signed attestations or other official literature from the manufacturer.

<u>Schools:</u>
- Acoustical elements within the building may require special installation considerations.
- The Collaborative for High Performance Schools (CHPS) Best Practices Manual, 206, Low-Emitting Materials (LEM) Table contains guidelines and strategies for effective acoustical performance in school buildings. Products listed are certified by the manufacturer and an independent laboratory to meet the CHPS LEM criteria.

Calculations: Na
Exemplary Performance: na
Construction Submittal
Timeline/Team: Requirements for IEQ Credit 4 (Low-Emitting Materials) should be noted in the project Specifications; clearly state credit requirements in the Specs.
Regional Variations: na
O&M Considerations: (1) Establish a sustainable purchasing policy (2) Provide operators with a list of compliant products. Use fewer composite wood or agrifiber products. Give operators information about specialty wood or agrifiber materials maintenance.

IEQ Credit 4.5 Low-Emitting Materials - Furniture and Furnishings (0, 0, 1*)

*Schools choose 4 credits from IEQ Credit 4.1 through IEQ Credit 4.6.

Intent (for Schools only): Reduce the quantity of indoor air contaminants that are odorous, irritating and/or harmful to the comfort and well-being of installers and occupants.

Requirements:

- Classroom furniture including all student and teacher desks, tables and seats that was manufactured, refurbished or refinished within 1 year prior to occupancy must meet 1 of the requirements below.
- Salvaged and used furniture that is over 1 year old at the time of occupancy is excluded from the credit requirements.

OPTION 1
- Furniture and seating must be **GREENGUARD Children and Schools** certified.

OPTION 2
- Calculated indoor air concentration contributions that are less than or equal to those listed in Table 1 for furniture systems and seating as determined by a procedure based on the **EPA** Environmental Technology Verification (ETV) Large Chamber Test Protocol for Measuring Emissions of VOCs and Aldehydes (Sept 1999) testing protocol conducted in an independent air quality testing laboratory.

Table 1. Maximum Indoor Air Concentrations

Architectural Applications	Classroom Furniture	Seating
Total VOCs	0.5 mg/m^3	0.25 mg/m^3
Formaldehyde	50 parts per billion	25 parts per billion
Total Aldehydes	100 parts per billion	50 parts per billion
4-Phenylcycohexene (4-PCH)	0.0065 mg/m^3	0.00325 mg/m^3

OPTION 3
- Calculated indoor air concentrations that are less than or equal to those established in Table 1 for furniture systems and seating as determined by a procedure based on **ANSI/BIFMA** M7.1-2007 and ANSI/BIFMA X7.1-2007 testing protocol conducted in an independent third party air quality testing laboratory.

LEED for Schools IEQ Credit 4 employs 3 approaches to limit off-gassing: (1) composition limits (2) emissions factors (3) performance based standards. For IEQ Credit 4.5, the performance-based standards approach is applied.

Performance Based Standards
- This analysis calculates the concentrations of each contaminant that each product will add to the air.
- In the selection of furniture systems and multiple office seating, confirm that the desired product will meet the testing requirements **when manufactured**.
- The Greenguard Environmental Institute provides a list of products that it has certified.
- Air velocity and outside air CFM should meet ASHRAE 62.1-2007.

Performance Based Emission Limits
- The product should not increase the concentration of contaminants in the air around it by any more than the threshold limits.
- The test chamber considers workstation size, mix of components and types of materials (including fabrics and finishes).

Implementation:
- Wooktools attached to furn., occasional furn., and salvaged furn. that is over 1 yr old at the time of occupancy are excluded.

Calculations: Na
Exemplary Performance: na
Construction Submittal
Timeline/Team: Requirements for IEQ Credit 4 (Low-Emitting Materials) should be noted in the project Specifications; clearly state credit requirements in the Specs.
Regional Variations: na
O&M Considerations: Establish a policy for continued use of low-emitting materials. Provide operators with a list of compliant products for repairs or alterations.

IEQ Credit 4.6 Low-Emitting Materials - Ceiling and Wall Systems (0, 0, 1*)

*Schools choose 4 credits from IEQ Credit 4.1 through IEQ Credit 4.6.

Intent (for Schools only): Reduce the quantity of indoor air contaminants that are odorous, irritating and/or harmful to the comfort and well-being of installers and occupants.

Requirements:

All gypsum board, insulation, acoustical ceiling systems and wall coverings installed in the building interior must meet the testing and product requirements of the California Department of Health Services Standard Practice for The Testing of Volatile Organic Emissions from Various Sources using Small-Scale Environmental Chambers, including 2004 Addenda.

Implementation:

Refer to IEQ Credit 4.1

Calculations: Na

Exemplary Performance: na

Construction Submittal

Timeline/Team: Requirements for IEQ Credit 4 (Low-Emitting Materials) should be noted in the project Specifications; clearly state credit requirements in the Specs.

Regional Variations: na

O&M Considerations: Establish a policy for continued use of low-emitting materials. Provide operators with a list of compliant products for repairs or alterations.

IEQ Credit 5 Indoor Chemical and Pollutant Source Control (1, 1, 1)

Intent: Minimize exposure of building occupants to potentially hazardous particulates and chemical pollutants.
Requirements:
Design to minimize and control pollutant entry into buildings and later cross-contamination of regularly occupied areas:

- Employ **permanent entryway systems** at least **10' long in the primary direction of travel** to **capture dirt and particulates** entering the building **at regularly used exterior entrances**.
- Acceptable entryway systems include permanently installed grates, grilles, or slotted systems that allow for cleaning underneath.
- Roll-out mats are only acceptable when maintained on a weekly basis by a contracted service organization.

- Where hazardous gasses or chemicals may be present or used (including garages, housekeeping/laundry areas and copying/printing rooms), <u>exhaust each space to create negative pressure</u> with respect to adjacent spaces <u>with</u> the <u>doors</u> to the room <u>closed</u>.
- For each of these spaces, provide <u>self-closing doors</u> and <u>deck-to-deck partitions or a hard lid ceiling</u>.
- The exhaust rate shall be at least <u>0.50 cfm/sq.ft., with no recirculation</u>.
- The pressure differential with the surrounding spaces shall be at least <u>-0.02" avg, -0.004" min</u> with the room doors closed.

- **In mechanically ventilated buildings, provide regularly occupied areas of the building with <u>new</u> air filtration media prior to occupancy, MERV 13 or better. Filtration should be applied <u>to process both return and outside air that is to be delivered as SA</u>. [ref ASHRAE 52.2]**

- Provide containment (closed container for storage for off-site disposal in a regulatory-compliant storage area, preferably outside the building) for appropriate disposal of hazardous liquid wastes in places where water and chemical concentrate mixing occurs for laboratory purposes.

Implementation:

- Design facility cleaning and maintenance areas with isolated exhaust systems for contaminants.
- Maintain physical isolation from the rest of the regularly occupied areas of the building.
- Install permanent architectural entryway systems such as grilles or grates to prevent occupant-borne contaminants from entering he building.
- Install high-level filtration systems in AHUs processing both RA and OA.
- Ensure that AHUs can accommodate required filter sizes and pressure drops.

Calculations: na

Exemplary Performance: na

Design Submittal

Timeline/Team: Design Team shall document equipment requirements and usage patterns. Architect should consider location and type of entryway system. Mechanical Engineer should incorporate MERV13 filters, dedicated exhaust systems, and dedicated drainage piping.

Regional Variations: Local weather determines location and type of entryway systems.

O&M Considerations: Replace filters and test/maintain exhaust systems. Establish a protocol for selecting, storing and handling hazardous waste. Develop, document and record entryway maintenance practices.

IEQ Credit 6.1 Controllability of Systems - Lighting (1, 1, 0)

Intent (for NC and Schools only): Provide a high level of lighting system control by individual occupants or by specific groups in multi-occupant spaces (e.g. classrooms and conference areas) to promote the productivity, comfort and well-being of building occupants.

Requirements:

NC:
- Provide **individual light controls** for a **minimum of 90% of the building occupants** to enable adjustments that suit the individual task needs and preferences.
- Provide **lighting system controls** for **all shared multi-occupant spaces** to enable adjustments that meet the group needs and preferences.

Schools:

CASE 1. Administration Offices and Other Regularly Occupied Spaces

- Provide **individual light controls** for a **minimum of 90% of the building occupants** to enable adjustments that suit the individual task needs and preferences.
- Provide lighting system controls for all learning spaces including classrooms, chemistry laboratories, art rooms, shops, music rooms, gymnasiums and dance and exercise studios to enable adjustments that meet group needs and preferences.

CASE 2. Classrooms

- Provide a lighting systems that operate in at least 2 modes:
     1. General illumination
     2. Audio/Visual

Implementation:

- Design the building with occupant controls for lighting.
- Strategies to consider include lighting controls and task lighting.
- Integrate lighting systems controllability into the overall lighting design.
- Provide uniform general ambient lighting with individually controlled task lighting (**consistent, ergonomic and operable**).
- Comply with ANSI/ASHRAE/IESNA 90.1-2007, task lighting; this should be included in lighting for EA Pr2 and Cr1.
- Daylighting can be integrated with this credit to compensate for reduced lighting intensity in IEQ Cr 8.1 and 8.2.
- If daylighting is used, glare control, lighting controls and room-darkening shades should be employed.
- **At a minimum, utilize ON/OFF task lighting control**; it is better to use multiple levels of control.

Calculations:
- Adjustable Task Lighting: Identify the workstations for individual use (private offices, open plan workstations, reception stations, ticket booths, etc). Confirm at least 90% of occupants have adjustable task lighting, e.g. ON/OFF, positioning, multiple levels, etc. **Task lights need not be permanently wired for LEED-NC.**

- Shared Multi-occupant Spaces: Specific types or numbers of controls are not listed in the Credit Requirements to allow for flexibility in designing to the unique uses of each project. Meeting spaces that can be subdivided, as with a movable wall in a convention hall, must be designed so occupants in each area have control of their area.

Exemplary Performance: na
Design Submittal
Timeline/Team: During Design – Architect or Lighting Designer consults with the owner to lay out lighting/controls and document the tasks specific to each space; involve Electrical Engineers; ensure whiteboards are free from glare; coordinate final calibration of the lighting controls with the installer and the Cx agent; train staff, review lighting systems and conduct an occupant survey.
Regional Variations: For regions with strong sunlight: consider daylighting, building orientation, canopies and daylight sensors.
O&M Considerations: Inventory number/type of controls installed; plan should include setpoints, schedules, & recalibration info.

IEQ Credit 6/6.2 Controllability of Systems - Thermal Comfort (1, 1, 1)

Note: (This Credit is called IEQ Credit 6 for Core & Shell because there is no IEQ Credit 6.1 for Core & Shell)

Intent: Provide a high level of thermal comfort system control by individual occupants or by specific groups in multi-occupant spaces (i.e., classrooms or conference areas) to promote the productivity, comfort and well-being of building occupants.

Requirements:

- Provide **individual comfort level controls** for a **minimum 50% of the building occupants** to enable adjustments to suit individual task needs and preferences. Operable **windows can be used in lieu of comfort controls** for occupants of **areas that are <u>20' inside of</u> and <u>10' to either side</u> of the operable part of the window**; the **minimum operable area** of the window **is 4% of 20'x20' area** (i.e., **16 sq.ft.**). The operable areas of the windows must meet the requirements of ASHRAE **62.1-2007, paragraph 5.1**, Natural Ventilation (with errata, without addenda).

- Provide **comfort system controls** for **all shared multi-occupant spaces** to enable adjustments to suit group needs and preferences.

- **Conditions for thermal comfort are described in <u>ASHRAE Standard 55-2004</u> (w errata, w/o addenda) to include the primary factors of <u>air T, radiant T, air velocity and RH</u>. Comfort system control, for the purposes of this credit, is defined as the provision of <u>control over at least one</u> of these primary factors in the occupant's local environment <u>(accepted by 80%).</u>**

<u>**Core & Shell IEQ Credit 6 (additional):**</u>

- C&S projects must purchase and/or install the mechanical system or operable windows (or a combination of both).
- See Appendix 1 – Default Occupancy Counts for occupancy count requirements and guidance.

Implementation:

- Design the building and systems with comfort controls to allow adjustments to suit individual needs or the needs of groups in shared spaces.
- ASHRAE 55-2007 identifies the primary factors of thermal comfort and a process for developing comfort criteria for spaces.
- Control strategies: operable windows, windows + mechanical systems, individual stats, local diffusers, local radiant panels.
- Evaluate interaction between thermal comfort (55-2007) and acceptable IAQ (62.1-2007).
- <u>Approved ASHRAE addenda may be used for this credit, but must be applied consistently across all credits</u>

Calculations:

- Confirm that **50% or more individuals** occupying these locations have at least one means of **individual comfort control over thermal comfort**.
- Confirm that operable windows with operable areas of 16 sq.ft. (per ASHRAE **62.1-2007 Section 5.1**) used in lieu of individual controls are located within 20' from and within 10 ' to either side of the operable part of the window (operable window area must be at least 4% of the net floor area, i.e. **20' x 20' x 4% = 16 ft^2**).
- For **shared multi-occupant spaces**, confirm that there is **at least one means of control over thermal comfort** that is accessible.

Exemplary Performance: na
Design Submittal
Timeline/Team: Consider building orientation and how heat gain or loss affects occupants; consider how wind, sound and other odors affect location of operable windows; after installation, the Cx should ensure proper operation; train staff and review comfort control systems periodically to ensure occupants' needs are met and that controls are working according to design.

Regional Variations: Local conditions affect the feasibility of operable windows, e.g. temperature, traffic, air pollution, etc.

O&M Considerations: Inform operators about the number and type of controls; the plan should include setpoints, schedules, recalibration procedures, specialty maintenance; replace filters more often if operable windows are used frequently.

IEQ Credit 7/7.1 Thermal Comfort - Design (1, 1, 1)

Note: (This Credit is called IEQ Credit 7 for Core & Shell because there is no IEQ Credit 7.2 for Core & Shell)

Intent: Provide a comfortable thermal environment that supports the productivity and well-being of building occupants.

Requirements:

- Design HVAC systems and the building envelope to meet the requirements of **ASHRAE Standard 55-2004 (with errata, without addenda)**, Thermal Comfort Conditions for Human Occupancy.
- Demonstrate design compliance in accordance with 55-2004 Section 6.1.1 (Documentation).

Schools (additional):

- For natatoriums, demonstrate compliance with the "Typical Natatorium Design Conditions" defined in Chapter 4 (Places of Assembly) of the ASHRAE HVAC Applications Handbook, 2004 edition (with errata but without addenda).

Core & Shell (additional):

- The C&S base building mechanical system must allow for the tenant build-out to meet the requirements of this credit.
- Project teams that design their project for mechanical ventilation but do not purchase or install the mechanical system are not eligible to achieve this credit.
- See Appendix 1 – Default Occupancy Counts for occupancy count requirements and guidance.

Implementation:

- Evaluate **air T, radiant T, air velocity and RH** in an **integrated design** and **coordinate** these criteria **with IEQ Pr1 and IEQ Cr1 and Cr2**.
- **ASHRAE 55-2004** (with errata, without addenda) requires that the **combination of thermal factors and personal factors** (clothing and activity) must be **acceptable to a minimum of 80%** of the occupants within a space.
- **ASHRAE 55-2004 is based on the Predicted Mean Vote (PMV) comfort model which is:**
    - based on a thermal sensation scale with **7 levels ranging from +3 (hot) to -3 (cold)**
    - applicable to **air speeds $\leq$ 40 fpm**.
- For **natural ventilation**:
    - Must consider outdoor climate
    - Chartered Institution of Building Services Engineers **(CIBSE) AM10 presents design strategies**
    - "Passive building, active occupants" applies, i.e. natural ventilation induces occupants to open/close windows
- Establish comfort criteria per 55-2004 that support desired quality and occupant satisfaction with building performance.
- Design building envelope and systems with the capability to deliver performance to the level of the comfort criteria under expected environmental and use conditions.
- Evaluate air T, radiant T, air velocity and RH in an integrated fashion and coordinate these criteria with IEQ Pr1, Cr1 and Cr2.
- Approved ASHRAE addenda may be used for this credit, but must be applied consistently across all credits

Calculations: Not required, but project teams should be able to describe how thermal comfort conditions were established and how the design of the conditioning systems addresses the thermal comfort design criteria.

Exemplary Performance: na
Design Submittal

Timeline/Team: Using 55-2004, the Design Team and Owner should identify systems and determine how to achieve thermal comfort; use load calculations to enable adequate capacity without oversizing; give occupants control to reduce complaints (**"passive buildings – active occupants",** i.e. occupants in naturally ventilated buildings actively open/close windows thereby taking a primary role in achieving thermal comfort).

Regional Variations: Consider climate and seasonal variations; warmer climates have higher design temperatures.

O&M Considerations: Educate the owner, maintenance staff and occupants (understand/maintain/adjust HVAC systems); the plan should include setpoints, schedules, corrective action, inspection, and calibration procedures.

IEQ Credit 7.2 Thermal Comfort - Verification (1, 1, 0)

Intent: Provide for the assessment of building thermal comfort over time.

Requirements:

NC and Schools:

- **Achieve IEQ Credit 7.1.**
- Implement an **anonymous thermal comfort survey (adults and students of grades 6 and above)** of occupants **within 6-18 months after occupancy**, including an assessment of overall satisfaction with thermal performance and an identification of comfort-related problems.
- Develop a **corrective action plan if** results indicate that **more than 20% of the occupants are dissatisfied**.
- The action plan should include measurement of the relevant environmental variables in problem areas in accordance with **ASHRAE Standard 55-2004 with errata, without addenda.**

NC (additional):

- Provide a **permanent monitoring system** to ensure building performance to the desired comfort criteria as determined by IEQ Cr 7.1, Thermal Comfort: Design.

- **Corrective action: measure/document relevant environmental variables in problem areas**, e.g. air T, radiant T, surface T, air velocity, RH, OAT, OARH, clothes, activity (per **ASHRAE Standard 55-2004 with errata, without addenda**).

- **Validate** building performance data and compare to **ASHRAE Standard 55-2004** criteria.

- **ASHRAE 55-2004 is based on the Predicted Mean Vote (PMV) comfort model which is:**

  - based on a thermal sensation scale with **7 levels ranging from +3 (hot) to -3 (cold)**
  - applicable to **air speeds ≤ 40 fpm**.

This credit is <u>not applicable to residential projects</u>.

This credit is <u>contingent on</u> the successful completion and award of <u>IEQ Credit 7.1</u>, Thermal Comfort: Design.

Implementation:

- Establish thermal comfort criteria and document/validate building performance according ASHRAE 55-2004.
- <u>55-2004 is not intended for continuous monitoring and maintenance of the thermal environment</u>, the <u>principles</u> expressed in the standard <u>provide a basis for</u> <u>design of monitoring and corrective action systems</u>.
- <u>Approved ASHRAE addenda may be used for this credit, but must be applied consistently across all credits.</u>

Calculations: na

Exemplary Performance: na

Design Submittal

Timeline/Team: Design Team is primarily responsible for achieving this credit (per 55-2004); a member of the building operations team, the owner's agent or a Cx should administer the survey.

Regional Variations: Consider climate and seasonal variations; warmer climates have higher design temperatures.

O&M Considerations: Educate the owner, maintenance staff and occupants (understand/maintain/adjust HVAC systems); the plan should include setpoints, schedules, corrective action, inspection, and calibration procedures.

IEQ Credit 8.1 Daylight and Views - Daylight (1, 1-3, 1)

Intent: Provide the building occupants a connection between indoor spaces and the outdoors through the introduction of daylight and views into the regularly occupied areas of the building.

Requirements:

<u>**Schools:**</u>
75% of classroom spaces	**1 point**
90% of classroom spaces	**2 points**
75% of other regularly occupied non-class spaces	**1 additional point (must achieve <u>at least 1</u> classroom space point)**

<u>**NC and C&S:**</u>
75% of regularly occupied spaces	**1 point**

OPTION 1 – SIMULATION

- Use a **computer simulation** to show that a **daylight illumination** level of **25-500 fc** has been achieved in a minimum of <u>**75% (NC, Schools, C&S)** or **90% (Schools only)**</u> of all **regularly occupied areas**.
- Use a horizontal calculation grid **30" above the floor or at the intended work plane; use maximum 5' grid intervals.**
- Model must show 25-500 fc under **clear sky, at 9 am and 3 pm, Sept 21**.
- Areas outside the 25-500 fc range do not comply; however, **use of view-preserving automated shades for glare control may demonstrate compliance for only the minimum 25 fc level.**

OPTION 2 – PRESCRIPTIVE

- **Achieve daylight illumination in at least <u>75% (1 point)</u> or <u>90% (2 points)</u> of all regularly occupied spaces.**
- Exceptions may be considered for areas where tasks would be hindered by the use of daylight.

<u>Sidelighting</u> Daylight Zone:
- o Multiply the visible light transmittance (VLT) times the window to floor area ratio (WFR) to achieve a daylight zone between 0.150 and 0.180, i.e. **0.150 < (VLT x WFR) < 0.180**
- o Window area included in the calculation must be of the portion of the window **at least 30" above the floor**.
- o **Ceiling should not obstruct a line in section** that joins the window-head to a point on a line (on the floor) that is twice as far from the window as the window-head is from the floor, i.e. **2H from the window if the H is the height of the window-head from the floor.**
- o Provide **sunlight redirection and/or glare control devices** to ensure daylight effectiveness.

<u>Toplighting</u> Daylight Zone:
- o The daylit zone **under a skylight** is the outline of the **opening beneath the skylight, plus** in each direction the **lesser of**:
    - **70% of the ceiling height**
    - **½ the distance to the edge of the nearest skylight**
    - **the distance to any permanent opaque partition (if transparent show VLT) that is farther away than 70% of the distance between the top of the partition and the ceiling**
- o Achieve a skylight roof coverage that is **3% to 6% of the roof area** with a **minimum 0.5 VLT** for the **skylights**.
- o The distance **between** the skylights shall **not be more than 1.4 times the ceiling height**.
- o Skylight must have a **diffuser** with a **measured haze value of greater than 90%** when tested per ASTM D1003.
- o Avoid direct line of sight to the skylight diffuser.

OPTION 3 - MEASUREMENT

- Show that a minimum daylight illumination level of **25 fc** has been achieved in <u>**≥ 75% (1 point)**</u> or <u>**90% (2 points)**</u> of all regularly occupied spaces.
- Use a 10' grid with measurements at 30" above the floor or at the work plane for the intended use of the space.
- Measurements must be taken for all occupied spaces and recorded on building floor plans.
- <u>Only</u> the square footage associated with the <u>portions of rooms/spaces meeting 25 fc</u> can be counted in the calculations.
- In all cases, provide glare control devices to avoid high-contrast situations that could impede visual tasks.
- Exceptions may be considered for areas where tasks would be hindered by the use of daylight.

OPTION 4 - COMBINATION

- Any of the above calculation methods may be **combined to document the minimum daylight illumination in at least 75% (1 point) or 90% (2 points) of all regularly occupied spaces.**
- In all cases, only the square footage associated with the portions of rooms or spaces meeting the credit requirements can be applied towards the total area calculation required to qualify for this credit.
- **In all cases, provide glare control** devices to avoid high-contrast situations that could impede visual tasks.
- Exceptions may be considered for areas where tasks would be hindered by the use of daylight.

VLT:	**Visible Light Transmittance:**	total transmitted light / total incident light
WFR:	**Window to Floor Area Ratio:**	window area / floor area
Geometric Factor:	effectiveness of a window to distribute daylight relative to window location	
Height Factor:	accounts for where light is introduced to the space	
Desk Height:	30" above finished floor	
<u>**Glare Control:**</u>	<u>most common problem in daylighting</u>	

Implementation:

- Design the building to maximize interior daylighting, e.g. orientation, shallow floor plates, increased perimeter, exterior and interior permanent shading devices, high performance glazing, high ceiling reflectance values, automatic photocell-based controls.
- Predict daylight factors via manual calculations or modeling (computer or physical) to assess fc levels and daylight factors.
- Glare control is perhaps the most common failure in daylighting strategies.

Calculations: see above

Exemplary Performance:
- <u>**NC and C&S**</u>: Daylight **95%** of regularly occupied spaces
- <u>**Schools**</u>: Daylight **90%** of all classrooms **and 95%** of all other regularly occupied non-classroom spaces

Design Submittal

Timeline/Team:
- Pre-design – Owner, Architect, Engineers
- Schematic Design – Architect, Civil Engineer, Landscape Architect
- Construction Documents – LEED calculations and/or computer model should be developed
- Construction – design and construction team review of submittals
- Occupancy – Owner should ensure no glare on occupants; facility manager should be advised of maintenance responsibilities

Regional Variations: Location and orientation issues include day length, sun path, and light availability.

O&M Considerations: Clean windows and shading; inspect sealants and flashings.

IEQ Credit 8.2 Daylight and Views - Views (1, 1, 1)

Intent: Provide the building occupants a connection between indoor spaces and the outdoors through the introduction of daylight and views into the regularly occupied areas of the building.

Requirements:
- Achieve **direct line of sight to the outdoor** environment via vision glazing between **30" and 90" above finish floor** for building occupants **in 90% of all regularly occupied areas**.
- Determine the area with direct line of sight by totaling the regularly occupied square footage that meets the following:
  - **In plan view**, the area is within direct sight lines drawn from perimeter vision glazing
  - **In section view**, a direct sight line can be drawn from the area to perimeter vision glazing
- Line of sight **may be drawn through interior glazing**.
- **Movable furniture and partitions are included** in the scope of this credit calculation.
- For **private offices, use entire area of the office if ≥ 75% of the area has direct line of sight to perimeter vision glazing**; **if < 75%, use the actual area** that has direct line of sight to perimeter vision glazing.
- For **multi-occupant spaces, only the actual area with direct line of sight** to perimeter vision glazing is counted.

Core & Shell (additional):
- The C&S design must incorporate a feasible tenant layout(s) per the default occupancy counts (or some other justifiable occupancy count) that can be used in the analysis of this credit.

Implementation:
- Design the space to maximize daylighting and view opportunities.
- Consider lower partition heights, interior shading devices, interior glazing, and automatic photocell-based controls.

Calculations:

DIRECT LINE OF SIGHT TO PERIMETER VISION GLAZING
1. From construction documents, create spreadsheet showing all regularly occupied rooms/areas and floor area of each.
2. From plan view, draw line of sight geometries at each window to determine the fraction of each regularly occupied room/area that has direct line of sight to the outdoors.
3. For private offices, use entire area of the office if > 75% of the area has direct line of sight to perimeter vision glazing (i.e. only the corners are non-compliant); if < 75%, use the estimated actual area.
4. For multi-occupant spaces, e.g. conference rooms, estimate the actual area with direct line of sight to perimeter vision glazing.

HORIZONTAL VIEW AT 42 INCHES
1. From plan view, draw a line at 42" (**average seated eye height**) across the section to establish the height of the perimeter glazing and obstruction to it. Draw one or more representative sight lines from a point at 42" within the regularly occupied space(s) to the perimeter vision glazing.
2. For each space where the view, taken 42" above the floor, is maintained, enter YES in the HORIZONTAL VIEW column of the spreadsheet. If a room has a direct line of sight in plan view but does not have an unobstructed view at 42", the floor area may not be counted and "NO" should be marked in the HORIZONTAL VIEW column.

BOTH: total the areas with **"YES" in the HORIZONTAL VIEW column** and divide by the total regularly occupied area.

Exemplary Performance: Meet 2 of the following 4 measures:
1. ≥ 90% of regularly occupied spaces have multiple lines of sight to vision glazing in different directions at least 90° apart.
2. ≥ 90% of regularly occupied spaces have views of at least 2 of: vegetation, human activity, or objects > 70' from the glazing.
3. ≥ 90% of regularly occupied spaces have access to unobstructed views located within 3 x head height of the vision glazing.
4. ≥ 90% of regularly occupied spaces have access to views with a view factor or 3 or greater.

Design Submittal
Timeline/Team: Schematic Design – Architect, Civil engineer, Landscape Architect should orient the building desireably. Identify regularly occupied spaces and locate them along the perimeter.

Regional Variations: Consider available duration and potency of sunlight and glazing heat loss or gain.

O&M Considerations: Clean windows and shading; inspect sealants and flashings; maintain landscaping.

IEQ Credit 9 Enhanced Acoustical Performance (0, 1, 0)

Intent (for Schools only):   Provide classrooms that facilitate better teacher-to-student and student-to-student communications through effective acoustical design.
Requirements:

Sound Transmission
- Design the building shell, classroom partitions and other core learning spaces to meet the Sound transmission class (STC) requirements of ANSI Standard S12.60-2002, Acoustical Performance Criteria, Design Requirements and Guidelines for Schools except windows, which must meet an **STC rating of at least 35**.

Background Noise
- Reduce **background noise level to 40 dBA** or less from HVAC systems in classrooms and other core learning spaces.

- **Background noise and reverberation** affect children, whose ability to distinguish sounds is not fully developed.
- Students are more likely to become distracted, have difficulty retaining information, and have trouble engaging in learning.
- Children with temporary hearing loss (15%), speech impairments and learning disabilities are especially affected.
- Planning for an effective acoustic environment improves teacher effectiveness, student performance and educational quality.
- Poor acoustics cause teachers' vocal fatigue and absenteeism, and students' remedial instruction and grade repetition.

Implementation
- To meet the requirements of this credit, designers need to consider 2 primary areas of performance:
    1. low background noise inside the core learning space
    2. appropriate sound isolation for core learning spaces from interior and exterior noise sources
- **Background noise is measured in dBA**, the A-weighted decibel sound pressure level measured on a non-linear scale.
- An increase of 10 dBA doubles the loudness, e.g. 90 dBA (jackhammer) is twice as loud as 80 dBA.(busy cafeteria)
- **Sound isolation is indicated by the STC rating** for sound attenuation properties of a wall, roof or other building element.
- A higher STC rating provides a higher level of sound attenuation.
- ANSI S12.60-2002 describes effective methods and strategies for HVAC noise control and sound isolation design.
- ASHRAE Chapter 47, 2007 HVAC Applications provides detailed methods for reducing noise transmission from HVAC
- **Exterior Background Noise**:
    - o Requirements are defined in S12.60-2002 as **STC ratings for exterior building elements**.
    - o A site with **outdoor noise levels $\geq$ 75 dBA may require additional control measures**, e.g. different orientation, sound barriers, and berms.
- **Interior Background Noise**:
    - o **HVAC equipment is usually the biggest source** of interior background noise.
    - o Do not install HVAC equipment near classrooms.
    - o Select quiet systems with central locations.
    - o Use simple ducting or acoustic duct liners.
- **Reverberation**:
    - o Replace existing low-NRC acoustical ceiling tiles with **high-NRC acoustical tiles**.
    - o Add new suspended acoustical tile (if height permits), or attach acoustical to the existing ceiling.
    - o Add sound-absorbing panels high on the walls at the sides and rear of room.
    - o If the classroom has a very high (over 11'), add acoustical panels on both ceiling and walls.
    - o **Carpet adds little to reverberation control** but is useful for controlling self-noise.
- **Sound Transmission**:
    - o Design classrooms to prevent transmission of sound from adjacent spaces through walls and ceilings.
    - o All construction elements in a room must **comply with the STC ratings listed in S12.60-2002**.

Calculations: see above for Background Noise and STC limits.
Exemplary Performance: achieve background noise level **55 dBA for playgrounds** and **60 dBA for athletic fields** and all other school grounds, or an **indoor noise level 35 dBA**.
Design Submittal
Timeline/Team: Schematic Design Phase – Coordinate with Mechanical Engineer, Electrical Engineer and Contractors; teachers & staff should educate Architects, Designers and Material Specifiers on the physical & spatial aspects of learning.
Regional Variations: Wind is an issue in the Midwest, fog and water vapor on the coast, natural ventilation everywhere.
O&M Considerations: Establish a policy for continued use of acoustical best practices during building operation; provide operators with a list of compliant products and materials for repairs or alterations.

IEQ Credit 10 Mold Prevention (0, 1, 0)

Intent (for Schools only): Reduce the potential presence of mold in schools through preventive design/construction measures.

Requirements:

- **Project teams must achieve the following Credits:**
    1. **IEQ Credit 3.1 Construction IAQ Management Plan – During Construction**
    2. **IEQ Credit 7.1 Thermal Comfort – Compliance**
    3. **IEQ Credit 7.2 Thermal Comfort – Verification**
- Provide HVAC systems and controls designed to limit space relative humidity to $\leq$ **60%** during **all load conditions**, both **occupied and unoccupied**.
- Develop and implement, on an ongoing basis, an IAQ management program for buildings based on the EPA document: **Building Air Quality: A Guide for Building Owners and Facility Managers, EPA reference number 402-F-91-102, December 1991.**

Implementation

- There are thousands of species of mold; **less than 10 are associated with chronic illness in the built environment**.
- Concentrations are measured in **Colony Forming Units (CFUs)**.
- Mold needs 3 things to grow: <u>oxygen</u>, <u>food</u> and <u>water</u>; water is the key.
- Address the following issues:
    1. Eliminate Potential for Condensation: keep RH at 60% or less.
    2. Pay Special Attention to Known Generators of Condensation: drain pans, drains, ducting.
    3. Prevent Mold During Unoccupied Periods.
    4. Address Floods and Leaky or Failed Equipment.
    5. Design for Mold Preventation.

Displacement Ventilation: Buoyancy driven airflow rather than forced airflow.
Mycotoxins: Toxic substances produced by fungi (mushrooms, molds, yeasts).
Dew Point: Temperature to which air must be cooled for the water vapor it contains to become liquid.

Calculations: na

Exemplary Performance: The project may be eligible for an ID point, but **there is no threshold**. Projects are evaluated on a case-by-case basis.

Design Submittal

Timeline/Team: Design Phase – Mechanical Engineer should identify and eliminate potential mold sources; the lead building engineer is responsible for ongoing efforts.

Regional Variations: Always an issue in warm, humid climates.

O&M Considerations: Consult with the owner and maintenance staff. The mold prevention plan should include setpoints/control sequencing, corrective action, procedures/schedules for preventative maintenance; designate the people responsible for implementing the ongoing IAQ management program and provide proper training and resources.

ID Credit 1 Innovation in Design `(1-5, 1-4, 1-5)`

Intent: To provide design teams and projects the opportunity to be rewarded points for <u>exceptional performance</u> above the requirements set by the LEED Green Building rating system <u>and/or</u> <u>innovative performance</u> in Green Building categories not specifically addressed by the LEED Green Building rating system.

Requirements:

Credit can be achieved through any combination of the following Paths:

PATH 1. Innovation in Design (1-5 Points for NC and C&S, 1-4 Points for Schools)
- Innovative performance in Green Building categories not specifically addressed by the LEED Green Building rating system
- One point is awarded for each innovation achieved
- **No more than <u>5 points for NC and C&S</u> or <u>4 points for Schools</u> may be earned through PATH 1.**
- Identify the following in writing:
    - o The intent of the proposed innovation credit
    - o The proposed requirement for compliance
    - o The proposed submittals to demonstrate compliance
    - o The design approach (strategies) that might be used to meet the requirements

PATH 2. Exemplary Performance (1-3 Points for NC, Schools, C&S)
- For a prerequisite or credit that allows Exemplary Performance, double the requirements and/or achieve the next incremental percentage threshold of an existing credit in LEED.
- One point is awarded for each Exemplary Performance achieved.
- **No more than 3 points may be earned through PATH 2.**

Innovation credits are not awarded for the use of a particular product or design strategy if the technology aids in the achievement of an existing LEED credit.

Approved ID credits may be pursued by any LEED project, but the project team must sufficiently document the achievement using the LEED credit equivalence process.

Examples of Innovation Credits
1. Educational program on the environmental and human health benefits of Green Building practices and how occupants or the public can help improve green performance.
2. Evaluate a substantial quantity of products and materials in the building based on an ISO14040 Life Cycle Assessment.
3. Expand waste diversion program to include waste from sources other than the building and grounds.
4. C&S projects can develop legally binding performance criteria for buyers/tenants to design and construct according to LEED.

ID Credit for Strategy Not Addressed by Existing LEED Credits
1. Demonstrate quantitative performance improvements for environmental benefit (establish baseline and final design).
2. The process or specification must be comprehensive, i.e. show that it applies to the entire project being certified.
3. The formula that is developed for the innovation credit must be applicable to other projects.

Calculations: Use calculation given within each LEED credit.

Documentation:
- Track development and implementation of the specific exceptional and innovative strategies used.
- For C&S projects, state the scope of the building that the innovation covers.

Timeline/Team: Innovation in Design should begin at project's conception, but it can enter at any step of the process and come from any project team member.
Regional Variations: Consider climate and regional architecture.

O&M Considerations: na

ID Credit 2 LEED Accredited Professional (1, 1, 1)

Intent: Support and encourage the design integration required by a LEED Green Building project. Streamline the application and certification process.

Requirements:

At least one principal participant of the project team must be a LEED AP.

Implementation:

1. Engage an individual within the organization who is already a LEED AP.
2. Hire a LEED AP to support the project.

Calculations: na

Construction Submittal:

Obtain confirmation from team members who are LEED APs or are planning to become LEED APs.

Timeline/Team: na

Regional Variations: na

O&M Considerations: na

ID Credit 3 The School as a Teaching Tool (0, 1, 0)

Intent: Integrate the sustainable features of a school facility with the school's educational mission.

Requirements:

- Design a curriculum based on the high-performance features of the building, and commit to implementing the curriculum **within 10 months of LEED certification**.
- The curriculum should not just describe the features themselves, but also explore the relationship between human ecology, natural ecology and the building.
- The curriculum must:
    1. meet local or state curriculum standards
    2. be approved by school administrators
    3. provide **10 or more hours of classroom instruction per year**, per full-time student.

- The curriculum may be designed as an **individual course or a component of other coursework**.
- The program heightens students' awareness of environmental issues.
- The program gives students a sense of ownership over their education.
- Hands on learning can lead to greater comprehension and retention of subject matter.

Examples of Learning Opportunities

- Water gardens
- Constructed wetlands
- Green roof or space
- Sundial
- Renewable energy systems
- Prominently displayed meters
- Visual and/or physical access to building infrastructure

Calculations: na

Documentation:

- Document the process by which the project team has worked to develop and/or implement the curriculum based on the high-performance features of the building.
- Maintain confirmation that the curriculum has been reviewed and approved by school administrators and meets applicable local and state curriculum standards.

Timeline/Team: Involve teachers early in the development of the curriculum; assess options for integrating the building into the curriculum.

Regional Variations: na

O&M Considerations: Maintain high-performance features; students may engage in O&M activities in some cases.

Regional Priority Credits: NC 2-6 Pts, Schools 3-6 Pts, C&S 2-6 Pts

RP Credit 1 Regional Priority (1-4, 1-4, 1-4)

Intent: To provide incentive for the achievement of credits that address geographically-specific environmental priorities.

Requirements:

- Achieve **up to four of the six** Regional Priority credits (credits identified as having **additional regional environmental importance** by the USGBC Regional Councils and Chapters **for the project's zip code**).
- A database of Regional Priority credits and their geographic applicability is available on the USGBC website.

One point is awarded for each Regional Priority credit earned, **up to a maximum of 4 RP credits**.

No more than 4 Regional Priority Credits will be awarded in the Regional Priority category.

Non-U.S. projects are not eligible for Regional Priority credits.

Calculations: na

Timeline/Team: Identify RP credits early in the project timeline.

Regional Variations: See "Regional Variations" under the particular RP credits **available for the project's zip code**.

O&M Considerations: See "O&M Considerations" under the particular RP credits **available for the project's zip code**.

LEED for Core & Shell: Tenant Lease or Sales Agreement

Overview:
- In a LEED C&S building, tenants can choose whether to pursue LEED for Commercial Interiors (CI) without affecting the building's LEED for C&S certification.
- However, if a developer **makes** technical requirements from the **LEED C&S** Rating System **part of a binding lease or sales**, the project may be able to earn additional points for credits with technical requirements not addressed in the C&S project design and construction scope.
- In other words, **C&S projects with a limited scope can achieve credits for activities that would otherwise be beyond their design and construction control by encouraging green building practices in the tenant's scope of work**.
- Compliance through a binding tenant lease or sales agreement can be pursued as an alternative to or in conjunction with the standard approach to C&S credit documentation.

Requirements:
- The technical credit requirements must be incorporated into a legally binding document signed by developer and tenant.
- The document must explicitly state performance requirements for the tenant work, e.g. lighting power density, plumbing fixture flow rates, or bike racks and showers.
- Guidelines, such as tenant design and construction guidelines required for SS Credit 9, and other nonbinding documents do not meet the requirements for this compliance method.
- **Only legally binding documents** satisfy the requirements of the Tenant Lease or Sales Agreement compliance method.

Documentation Guidance:
- Submit sample agreements when applying for precertification as well as certification.
- For specific documentation requirements, refer to the selected credits in LEED Online.

Applicable Credits:

CASE A:
- Documentation for CASE A credits must include data from the entire project building, including tenant-occupied spaces.
- Project teams should treat anticipated tenant work as neutral, or, if claiming performance improvements based on anticipated tenant work, the improvements must be supported by tenant sales and/or lease agreements.
    - WE Prerequisite 1
    - WE Credit 3
    - EA Prerequisite 2
    - EA Credit 1 (performance path only)

CASE B:
- Submittal documentation for CASE B credits need only include data from the C&S project scope.
- If the project team wishes to claim performance improvements based on anticipated tenant work, the improvements must be supported by tenant sales and/or lease agreements.
    - WE Credit 2
    - EA Credit 2

CASE C:
- Submittal documentation for CASE C credits must include data from the entire project building.
- In some cases, the C&S project will be limited such that compliance cannot be documented without including data from anticipated tenant work. In these cases, such data must be supported by tenant sales and/or lease agreements.
    - SS Credit 4.2
    - EA Prerequisite 3
    - EA Credit 4
    - IEQ Prerequisite 1
    - IEQ Credit 1
    - IEQ Prerequisite 2
    - IEQ Credit 2
    - IEQ Credit 5
    - IEQ Credit 6

C&S Tenant Lease or Agreement (cont.)

Exemplary Performance: Earn ID points by requiring tenants to achieve exemplary performance in certain credits.

- Achieve the credit requirements for C&S submittal.
- Provide documentation and meet the requirements of the Tenant Lease or Sales Agreement compliance paths.
- Exemplary performance under Tenant Lease or Sales Agreement is available for the following credits:
    - SS Cr8: Light Pollution Reduction: automatic controls within 100% of the tenant spaces.
    - EA Cr2: On-site Renewable Energy: tenant must achieve 5% on-site renewable energy.
    - IEQ Cr3: Construction IAQ Management Plan: tenant must adhere to a construction IAQ management plan.
    - IEQ Cr4: Low-emitting Materials: tenant must comply with IEQ Credits 4.1-4.4 throughout the tenant space.

LEED for Core & Shell: Precertification Guidance

Overview:

- Precertification is formal recognition by GBCI that the owner or developer has established LEED for C&S as a goal.
- It is unique to C&S and may be pursued at the project team's discretion.
- It gives C&S building owners and developers a marketing tool to attract potential tenants and financiers.
- It occurs early in the design process and is based on intent to use green features, not actual achievement of these features.

Process:

- After project registration, the project team may apply for precertification.
- Precertification is not certification or the promise of certification.
- The documentation and review processes are less comprehensive than for a full certification application.
- The documentation requirements differ in that they are focused on verification of design intentions rather actions.
- The review occurs in two phases: preliminary review and final review.
- After preliminary review, the team has a chance to respond to initial review comments and update any documentation as necessary.
- Precertification can be awarded at the project's expected certification level (Certified, Silver, Gold or Platinum).
- A project for precertification receives a certificate and letter.

BUY THE REFERENCE GUIDE!
LEARN GUIDE GLOSSARY!!!